How You Can Play
Better Golf
Using Self-Hypnosis

Jack G. Heise

Author of

"How You Can Bowl Better
Using Self-Hypnosis"

Published by
Melvin Powers
WILSHIRE BOOK COMPANY
12015 Sherman Road
No. Hollywood, California 91605
Telephone: (213) 875-1711 / (818) 983-1105

Copyright
1961

Wilshire Book Company

Printed by

HAL LEIGHTON PRINTING COMPANY
P.O. Box 3952
North Hollywood, California 91605
Telephone: (213) 983-1105

Library of Congress Catalog Card Number: 60-53323
Printed in the United States of America
ISBN 0-87980-073-9

ILLUSTRATIONS

TROUBLE SHOTS

Here is a player exhibiting the technique of recovering from a sand trap. Note the apparent ease of the swing. He has not allowed conscious fear to create tension in the muscle movements. Fear-produced tensions cause "freezing." Self-hypnosis enables you to conquer conscious fear when you are faced with trouble shots.

PUTTING FEARS

Even the experts are sometimes thwarted by "jitters" on the putting green, which are uncontrolled fears influencing muscle action. Self-hypnosis, which provides an explanation of the relationship between the conscious and subconscious mind, reveals how these fears are created and how they can be kept in control.

CONCENTRATION AND RELAXATION

Here is an excellent example of what the experts mean when they say the golfer must concentrate and yet be relaxed. Note, the attention is focused on the ball, while there is no hint that the muscles have become tense. It is through self-hypnosis that the dual state of concentration and relaxation can be combined to produce the correct golf swing.

EYES ON THE BALL

The controversial subject as to whether the eyes must be kept on the ball and the head down during impact is well illustrated in this photo. The player has not "forced" this position. It is a natural result of concentration of the conscious mind upon the ball, while the subconscious mind automatically controls the rest of the movements in the swing.

FOLLOW-THROUGH

Here is a picture showing excellent follow-through. It is evidence of how well the stroke has been "grooved." Note the player's relaxed muscles at the finish of the swing. This relaxed position is only possible when the stroke has been played with the muscles controlled by the subconscious mind.

CONTENTS

Chapter 1

HERE IS A PROMISE FOR BETTER GOLF

Why is it that the good golfer appears to hit the ball with such ease, while the duffer, "giving it everything he's got," appears to be using a rubber-shafted club and a steel ball?

Have you ever strewn divots all the way around a course while concentrating on the theories of the straight left arm, steady head, hip turn and right elbow down? You know all there is to know about the mechanics of the golf swing and can recite the theories forwards and backwards. The only thing you don't understand is your score. It seems the more you know and the harder you try, the worse you get.

If it is true that you know the fundamental movements of the golf stroke yet fail to play well, your failure must be in your mental play.

"And just what," you ask, "is mental play?" Let's go to the experts to see what they have to say.

"The average individual," says sports writer Grantland Rice, "has given almost no attention to mental control, which in golf should be an absence of conscious thinking as the stroke is played." Psychologists call this automatic mastery a conditioned reflex.

"The subconscious mind is probably the most important factor in being a good golfer. It keeps distractions on the course from ruining a good round. You should practice, develop your swing, and do most of your thinking on the practice tee so that when you play in competition, you can hit the ball automatically." That's what Wiffy Cox, the nationally known pro at the Congressional Golf and Country Club in Bethesda, Maryland, has to say about it.

"Trouble shots are surprisingly easy if you activate your imagination. You simply must be able to imagine exactly what flight the ball will take before you can play any shot well," advises the great Walter Hagen.

The great "Slammin' Sam" Snead writes: "First and foremost, you must have confidence. Your second mental problem is concentration. Think the shot through in advance before you address the ball. Draw a mental image of where you want it to go and then eliminate everything else from your mind, except how you are going to get the ball into that preferred spot."

The experts have spoken! The only problem is that they have told you what you must do, but left out instructions on how to do it. What do they mean by "Do most of your thinking on the practice tee," "Activate your imagination,"

"A fairly blank mind, after the backswing has started, is a great help," "Eliminate everything else from your mind," "Absence of conscious thinking"?

As you can see, most of the instructions on the mental approach to golf are so vague they are difficult to understand.

One of the reasons why professionals who sincerely attempt to share their knowledge of the game with less proficient players are thwarted is because they grew up with the game. As caddies, they developed their golf swing and golf thinking at an early, formative age. They learned to play by imitating good players. The facility to learn through imitation is reserved almost exclusively for youth.

When a person reaches maturity his conscious mind develops its true function: to question, to doubt, to challenge all facts presented to it. It demands to know the reason for all actions, thereby eliminating the ability to imitate without question.

An infant feeds himself, walks and talks by imitation. A youth learns to swim, ride a bicycle, or swing a golf club by imitation. No question is asked, so long as the action produces the desired results.

Instructions for an adult must not only include being shown or told what to do, but must contain a reasonable explanation as to how and why it should be done in that way.

Another stumbling block for instruction on mental play has been that it is often given in terms of what the student should do, rather than how he should do it. This is a statement of effect, rather than cause.

BETTER GOLF USING SELF-HYPNOSIS

The difference between the good player and the poor player is his mental approach to both the swing and the game. The good player knows not only what to think, but how to utilize his thought to make his play effective. The poor player, unable to visualize such terms as concentration, blank mind, relaxation and tension, struggles hopelessly in a mental fog. He is like the person who owns a telephone, radio or television set. He knows there are certain mechanical parts that are operated by electricity. However, without complete instructions he could not put one together and make it operate, even if he had all the parts.

The instruction for assembling the mechanical parts of the swing is the mental side of golf. The power to operate it is hypnosis.

Should the term hypnosis connotate mystery, black magic, stage trickery or fear, disregard it. Upon closer examination, you will find you are not only familiar with it, but have been using it while thinking of it in other terms such as self-discipline, positive thinking, automatic response, muscle memory, suggestion or unconscious desire.

Hypnosis is not a new phenomenon. Its recorded history goes much further back in time than that of the ancient and honorable game of golf. Whereas some authorities claim golf originated with the early Romans in a sport they called "Paganica," references to hypnosis have been found on stone tablets, unearthed in Greece, dating back to 3000 B.C.

The only thing new about hypnosis is when you, yourself, become aware of it. Then, its great power to influence the mind becomes known to you. You will learn to use it effectively, because you will understand how to channel its forces to tap the hidden resources of your subconscious mind.

Hypnosis, like the golf stroke, to the uninitiated is a mystery, not so much in what it is, but in how it is accomplished. Every good golfer, whether he recognizes the phenomenon as such, employs self-hypnosis in his play. Realization of this fact and an understanding of the relationship between the conscious and subconscious mind will inevitably result in better golf.

Would you like to curb that "killer instinct" off the tee? Would you like to thaw that psychological freeze when faced with hazards, cure the "jitters" on the putting green, and put both power and direction in your shot-making? This is what you may expect by applying self-hypnosis to your play.

In order to reach these goals, it is necessary to assimilate the directions step by step. You must promise to treat this book as you would a mystery thriller, by not peeking ahead to find the answer sooner. Unless prepared by an understanding of the process involved, the induction of self-hypnosis may seem so easy that you may find it difficult to believe such amazing results are possible with so little effort. The study of hypnosis is similar to a course in higher mathematics, in which deduction, analysis and logic are sought, rather than the obvious answer.

The request to follow the pages in order is not made for the purpose of impressing upon you that a great, new, and secret discovery has been made. Rather, it is to instruct you in self-hypnosis in order to improve your golf score. Proof will be found in your own lowered handicap.

Book stores and libraries have racks filled with volumes on physical golf. Analysis of the play of champions, back to the time James I paired with his cobbler to wrest the title from the Stuart Clan in the sixteenth century, is dealt with in detail.

Autobiographies by professionals reveal, with the frankness of confession story writers, how they "feel" during every movement. Doctors have written golf books dissecting the swing, with detailed descriptions of each part of the anatomy involved.

Theorists treat the aesthetic qualities of both golf and golfers with nuances usually reserved for poetry. Endless "tips" appear in newspapers and magazines aimed at improving the game of the average player.

You will probably agree that any further discussion on the physical side of golf was precluded when the champion of champions, Ben Hogan, published his informative *Five Lessons* — with illustrations by Ravielli. It shows every movement of bone and muscle that the game of golf brings into play and is worthy of being a surgeon's manual.

Why are there so many players seriously seeking improvement when the golf swing has been so completely revealed, charted, and plotted with the thoroughness of a geographical map? Why do they find it so difficult to hack their way around the course under 100 strokes? What keeps them from breaking 90, or coming close to par?

If it is true that the average player knows the fundamental movements of the golf stroke, yet fails to play well, it must follow that his failure is in his mental play.

HERE IS A PROMISE FOR BETTER GOLF

Through hypnosis, the way to obtain a mental effect may be explained, understood, and put to use. It reveals the mental side of golf with the clarity that high speed cameras disclose the physical movements of the golf swing.

Prior to "magic eye" photography, many fallacies existed concerning the golf stroke. These errors were made by the players when they attempted to describe what they thought they were doing. Only when stop-motion cameras were used was proof as to how they were doing it finally established. Just as these cameras were used to prove the mechanics of golf, so does hypnosis give proof as to how the champions think.

If you have studied numerous books on how to play golf, you probably reached the conclusion that either all of these books were written by the same ghost writer or that there is only one correct way to swing a golf club. Close study of the professional form in sequence photographs shows conclusively that there is only one way to swing the golf club. To be effective, it must follow a certain path to contact the ball in order to propel it any distance in a straight line. In golf, the shortest distance to par is a straight line.

Should you have any doubt that there is only one correct mechanical stroke, take a piece of tracing paper and outline the basic movement of the champions from their sequence pictures. You will find that one will fit over the other. The only variance will be the physical difference in their height and weight.

The golf swing is physical. It is performed mechanically by the use of muscles. However, all muscle movement, both conscious and subconscious, is controlled by the mind. Self-hypnosis allows both the conscious and subconscious minds to perform their separate duties with a minimum of effort for the best results.

In the popular King Features syndicated newspaper column, "Mirror of Your Mind," the question was asked of Joseph Whitney: "Can hypnosis improve your golf game?"

He answered: "Properly performed, hypnosis is capable of changing mental attitudes at the conscious level. If faulty mental attitudes are responsible for a golfer's inadequate performance, a change wrought by hypnosis could help him improve his skill."

Dr. Conrad Gayle, New York City, Diplomate of the American Board of Hypnosis, said recently, "Hypnosis cannot correct the basic mechanism involved, for example, a golfer's slice, but it can make it easier for him to learn to correct his slice by relaxing tensions at the conscious level."

Through the use of self-hypnosis, you will learn to relax your tensions at the conscious level, allowing the subconscious to assume its power role in the golf swing. This alone produces the automatic grooved swing of the champions.

Remember, conscious effort is a swing-wrecker!

Subconscious control is the par maker!

Chapter 2

THE SIX-INCH COURSE

Most amateur golfers are bitten (and infected beyond cure) by the golf bug after they become adults.

The age of imitation has long passed. They attack their game as adults. They research it deeply by reading every book on how to play golf they can find. Then, they go out on the course and practice diligently. They even take instructions from a teaching professional, thinking this is all they have to do to master the game. Well, is it?

Remembering everything you have ever read about the mechanics of golf, do you still find yourself hooking and slicing on the course until you feel like wrapping your club around a tree?

After a thoroughly exasperating game you go home, and there on the sports page is a "tip" from one of the masters telling you exactly what to do to correct a slice. What he says sounds pretty reasonable, so forgetting how tired you are (and ignoring your wife's call to dinner) you pick up your clubs and balls and head for the back yard.

With considerable danger to the grass, you imitate what you have just read in slow motion. You continue practicing until the thought strikes you, "I can't see myself, so how do I know I'm doing it right?"

Then, it comes to you. There is a full length mirror in your bedroom that was made for just this sort of emergency. Closing your mind to your wife's threat she'll divorce you if you harm her beautiful mirror, you pass her with a muttered, "Well, it's my house, too."

What's the matter with women? Don't they know that a mirror is an excellent means of checking such highly important movements as knee bend, hip turn, and steady hand?

There you stand looking at yourself and thinking, "After reading all those books by the professionals, I feel I know how to use every golf muscle. I am confident that with a little intelligent application I can duplicate the swing of the pros."

So you practice, and practice, and practice, and practice. First, you do it slowly. Then, you gradually speed it up until you just know that you've got it.

Black despair engulfs you the next day when your new technique fails to stand up under the pressure of real play. For some elusive reason, the "fool-proof" form depicted in the bedroom mirror deserts you on the course.

This is the point at which you find yourself at night, after hours of wakeful contemplation upon your golfing faults, flinging yourself from bed to practice your swing in the living room. Returning to bed, you find that sleep finally comes with the sweet assurance that at long last you have found the "secret."

This feeling immediately deserts you when your handicap increases six strokes.

There is no more persistent breed than the amateur golfer.

Determined to find the answer, you will read and re-read Tommy Armour, Ernest Jones, Jack Burke, and Ben Hogan. There will be times when, with hope high, you climb slowly down the handicap ladder. It will be dashed when, just as things seem to be going well, you falter again.

Physically, you feel capable of accomplishing the movements so graphically described by the experts. Mentally, you are confused by your failure. The most humbling experience you will ever have is to go to a women's professional tournament and see wisps of girls half your size hit the ball twice as far.

At this point, you return to your teaching pro.

You review his instruction, and graciously offer him all the "tips" you have picked up during your research. You hit a bucketful of balls, and, like the fellow whose pain mysteriously disappears as he enters the doctor's office, the slices and scuffs vanish.

"There is nothing basically wrong with your swing," he says. "Your only trouble is that you try too hard. You know what you're supposed to do, but you can't do it in competition because you're trying to 'murder' every shot."

His explanation leaves you completely baffled. How

can you possibly keep from trying hard to do something you desperately wish to accomplish? Didn't Tommy Armour advise you in his book to hold the club in the left hand and whack hell out of the ball with the right?

You put your questions to the pro, and he tries to explain what he said in a different way. "You'll have to force yourself to swing easy while you're playing."

This instruction, difficult as it is to follow —"to try hard," "not to try too hard," and "swing easy"— manages to compound bad shots without distance. Your handicap again goes up.

"It has to be mental," you tell yourself. Now, you return to your golf books to find out what they have to say concerning the mental side of the game.

This creates real confusion. On the physical side of golf, except for minor divergents as to grip and stance, the pros appear in agreement. On the mental side of the game, there seems to be no less than a dozen different, and often diametrically opposed, views.

Some professionals insist the player must "concentrate on the stroke to the exclusion of everything else." Others claim the swing should be made "with a blank mind." There is talk of "being intent upon the target" while at the same time the player is supposed to be "completely relaxed in body and mind." There are discussions of tensions, frustrations, golf gremlins, voices within, and mental pictures.

What appears to be near "mystic" is the claim of some professionals that they can hook or slice by merely thinking "hook" or "slice." One famous English pro says he thinks he can "will the ball in the hole."

Each theory is stated positively. You are admonished to follow directions explicitly. But nowhere can you find an explanation of just how to accomplish these near miraculous feats.

You try your best to keep a mental picture of the ball in flight and at the same time remember to hold the left arm firm, the right elbow down, and the head steady. You admit complete defeat after trying to do this while "keeping the mind blank."

Unbelievable as it may seem to you, each of these instructions is completely valid.

In fact, every one of them is a must for good golf.

A good golfer must have a mental picture of both the golf swing and the flight of the ball. He must be intent upon making a shot while relaxed. He must remember the basic movements of the swing while the mind is blank. Furthermore, he can do all these things simultaneously through the use of self-hypnosis.

The obscurity of the instruction is in accepting the role played by the conscious and subconscious minds. Until you learn about hypnosis, you will probably classify the mind as singular. When you acquire an understanding of the functions of the conscious and subconscious minds, most of your golfing troubles are over.

"Much of anyone's game is played (or should be played) in the short six-inch course between the ears," said Louise Suggs, winner of both the American and British Open Crowns.

Even after you have been over a course many times, it

isn't an easy layout to play, because most of the hazards are created by yourself.

Willie Ogg, instructor at the Professional Golfers Association school in Dunedin, Florida, lecturing on "Tensions and the Psychological Freeze," put it this way:

"One touch of jitters makes all golfers kin.

"The ideal is reached when one has only to think of mechanical control for the mechanical action. This is a matter of inducing self-hypnosis or complete concentration."

However, there is that little matter of knowing how to maintain an "absence of conscious thought while making the stroke."

The conscious mind cannot be turned off and on like a water faucet, except through hypnosis.

"The subconscious mind is probably the most important factor in being a good golfer. It keeps distraction on the course from ruining a good round," said Wiffy Cox.

This is the essence of self-hypnosis. Hypnosis distracts the conscious mind and allows the subconscious to function. Through self-hypnosis comes the "subconscious feel." It is attained in the practice area as a measure for every shot. When you have this subconscious feel, then your swing becomes automatic.

While playing in Seattle, Washington, one year, I met Woodrow Auge, a businessman.

Auge is in his 40's, husky, powerfully built, and keeps himself in top physical condition. We met as he was playing his first game "since fooling around a bit with it in high school."

THE SIX-INCH COURSE

It wasn't unexpected that he scored 126 on a par 72 course. He was a doomed man. The golf bug had bitten him, because he said, "You know, I think I'll take up golf. I've been spending my summers playing soft ball with one of our store teams, but it's a kid's game and getting too tough. I like the sociability of golf."

Auge returned to the course the following week. By dint of overpowering the ball, he cut his score by four strokes.

"I'm buying a set of clubs," he told me. "How about going to the driving range some evening and giving me a few pointers? It's been so long since I played, I've forgotten everything I knew, except how to keep score. And at the rate I'm going, I'll need an adding machine for that."

I asked Auge if he would mind being a guinea pig for an experiment. A number of other players I knew were using self-hypnosis, but they were experienced in the mechanical movements of the game. He would be the first who might be classified as a beginner to put the theory to a test.

"I have nothing to lose," Auge said gamely. "I'll string along with whatever you say if you think I can get to play well enough to make the game interesting."

In exactly three months, Woodrow Auge broke 80!

Much of the credit for his remarkable feat must be given to his splendid physical condition and a real determination to master the game. He played often, and spent evenings at the driving range. However, I think it may stand as a near record for a person to start almost from scratch and drop 48 strokes to score a 78 in three months.

Auge credits the instruction he received on self-hypnosis, which explained the mental side of golf to him, for his rapid improvement.

"I don't care whether it is in business or golf," he said, "a fellow isn't going anywhere until he knows what he is doing. Once I got it through my head about controlling the golf swing with the subconscious mind, the rest came easy."

If Auge, an amateur just like you, can lower his score 48 points by using self-hypnosis, why can't you?

Chapter 3

YOUR SUBCONSCIOUS
AND ITS APPLICATION
FOR BETTER GOLF

Hypnosis can be explained best by what it can do and how it is accomplished, rather than by what it is. The phenomenon of hypnosis is recognized by both the American and British Medical Associations. That, in itself, should constitute documentation for even the most skeptical.

The cause of hypnotic phenomenon is still controversial, but a majority of authorities concur in the theory that hypnotism is a state of heightened suggestibility which enables an individual to make appropriate responses. It is accomplished by distracting the conscious mind from a multitude of thoughts and concentrating it upon a single object or thought, so direct contact may be made with the subconscious mind.

What hypnotism can do is well authenticated. Clinical reports fill volumes in medical libraries. Physicians have used it for painless childbirth, surgery and alleviation of pain without chemical analgesia. Psychiatrists have found it a useful tool to uncover repressed or guarded secrets of the mind. They also employ it with great success in psychotherapy for the mentally ill.

Hypnosis is not only for the sick and emotionally disturbed. As stated by Dr. Frank S. Caprio, an eminent Washington psychiatrist, "It may be used by the normal person to relieve tensions, inspire confidence and add zest to living."

The word "hypnosis" derives from the Greek word "hypnos," meaning sleep. It was coined by an English physician, Dr. James Braid, in the 18th century. Later, Dr. Braid recognized his error and stated that while hypnosis resembled sleep, it is not normal sleep, and, in fact, quite the opposite in many ways. He attempted, unsuccessfully, to change the name to "monoideism," to signify it was due to being engrossed with a single idea.

Today, authorities agree hypnosis is akin to concentration which excludes all but the desired stimuli, but it cannot be completely explained by this theory. It has been proved that Dr. Braid was correct in assuming there was no relationship to sleep other than a superficial resemblance. The electroencephalograph (a machine for measuring brain waves) has shown brain frequencies during hypnosis are similar to those in the waking state, differing considerably from those during sleep.

If you are coming into contact with hypnosis for the first time, you should be aware of two points concerning its usage.

First, a person who can be hypnotized is not "weak willed." On the contrary, the hypnotist is merely the "instrument" through which you are able to reach a state of hypnosis. Actually, you hypnotize yourself, the power being supplied by your own intelligence and concentration.

"A hypnotized patient is never in anybody else's power. He won't go into a trance unless he wants to. He won't do anything unless he wants to. And he won't stay in a trance if he wants to come out of it." This statement was made by Dr. Roy M. Dorcus, professor of psychology at the University of California at Los Angeles.

Second, there is no danger that you will not awaken from a hypnotic trance. In all the recorded history of hypnosis there is not a single instance in which a subject failed to return to the normal waking state.

"Self-hypnosis plays a valuable role in a process which makes it easier for an individual to discover and understand the workings of his own body and mind, learn the factors which basically cause his own distress, and learn how to control them." This complete description of the phenomenon of self-hypnosis was given by Dr. Milton Erickson, dean of the American medical hypnotists.

Applying Dr. Erickson's words to golf, you may use self-hypnosis to learn the basic movements of the golf swing (understanding the workings of your own body and mind), and at the same time learn what causes the tensions during play and how to control them.

Instruction given by professional golfers is sincere and sound advice. Through the use of self-hypnosis, you will understand it more clearly and be able to use it more effectively.

Sir Walter Simpson, in his book, *The Art of Golf,* published in England in 1887, said, "There is only one categorical imperative in golf and that is to hit the ball. There are no minor absolutes."

You can't take issue with that statement, because it *is* necessary to hit the ball. The problem confronting you is to hit it well enough to get it into the hole in near regulation figures.

An oft-quoted instruction from "Slammin' Sam" Snead is, "My idea of playing golf has always been to play it as simply and naturally as possible."

There is no doubt that Samuel Jackson Snead plays his game that way. He started swinging a club when he was a barefoot caddy at the Homestead course in Hot Springs, Virginia. By the time Sam was 20, he was a professional. Five years later, in 1932, he won the Los Angeles Open.

He is also a good example of a professional who started early enough in life to use the art of imitation. The mechanical movements of golf were powerfully impressed on his subconscious mind at an early age, so that now, as an adult, his play is simple, natural, and, most of all, automatic.

He is trying to explain this subconscious feel when he tells you, "First and foremost, you must have confidence. Your second mental problem is concentration. Think the shot through in advance before you address the ball. Draw a mental image of where you want it to go and then eliminate everything else from your mind . . ."

Forming a mental picture is one phase of self-hypnosis in which you will receive instruction. But until you learn how to transfer the mental image in the conscious mind to subconscious feel, you may find it difficult to follow his advice to "eliminate everything else from your mind."

Just as a test, try right now to see how long you can hold a single thought in your mind before other thoughts interfere.

Hard to do, isn't it?

Psychologists explain this phenomenon by saying that the conscious mind is in a constant state of flux. Without the assistance of hypnosis, it is impossible to center its attention upon any one thought or object for any period of time.

It is the difference between knowing what to do and knowing how to do it that separates the professional from the average player. "The greatest difference between the star and the average player," said Walter Hagen, "is the way they handle the bunkers, pits, and rough.

"Part of this is mental. Most of it is. The star knows he is pretty sure to be out in one stroke, so he doesn't worry much.

"The duffer doesn't know how long he may be in the pit or trap.

"As a result, the star takes a natural grip, doesn't tighten too much, doesn't hurry the stroke, and lets fly with confidence."

Could this be the old question of the chicken or the egg? If it takes confidence to acquire ability, and ability to inspire confidence, where is the beginning or end of the circle?

Hagen's great confidence is typified by his mental approach to the big matches. Taking his stance on the first tee, he would wink to his partisan gallery and ask, "I wonder who will be second in this one?"

Haven't you found that when you are on a tee with an out-of-bounds marker to the left, a wooded rough on the right, and you are trying to remember straight left arm, elbow down, and head steady — confidence is hard to come by?

Yet without confidence you cannot play good golf. Without confidence, there is fear. Fear produces muscle tension. Muscle tension wrecks the golf swing.

You can acquire confidence through self-hypnosis by learning to rely upon your subconscious feel, which has been referred to by the experts as the "don't think" or "blank mind" theory for golf.

In his book, *The Natural Way to Better Golf,* Jackie Burke relates an incident in which he asked a well-known pro what he thought about when he hit the ball. The answer was, "Nothing."

Burke, who claims he has used a hundred dozen golf balls, worn out twelve pairs of golf shoes, and walked 18,000 miles on the pro trail, says that "thinking of nothing" is the only way to relax the body and mind while making the golf shot.

This advice, once you recognize the golf swing must be controlled by an automatic reflex from the subconscious mind, is exactly what you need. But until you know how to employ the power of subconscious control, trying to consciously "think of nothing" may lead to all kinds of trouble.

The point, as psychologists have determined, is that so long as the conscious mind is aware a penalty is involved in any action, it cannot be avoided by an act of will but only through hypnosis.

Chick Hart offered an explanation for the "blank mind" theory when he wrote: "As you have noted, knowing the fundamentals of the golf swing is primary, but to constantly repeat them over every shot is not the answer to consistent golf.

"I have a strong feeling the top pros concentrate on one thing and then rely upon the subconscious feel for playing their shots. The fact that it is not so described by them may be because that for them it is such a natural talent.

"To say that an especially difficult shot was made by thinking of nothing, to me shows only that the player may not have been aware he was practicing the principle of good mental play by employing the subconscious feel."

The subconscious feel is explained when you know the relationship between the conscious and subconscious mind.

Ernest Jones, the respected golf writer and teacher, recognized this in his book, *Swing The Clubhead*. He might well have become another Bobby Jones if he had not been wounded during World War I, the result being the loss of his right leg. Two months after the operation, Jones swung his way around a golf course on crutches and scored an 83. Later, with an artificial leg, he won the prized Kent Cup.

Due to his physical limitation, Jones learned the importance of balance and the true meaning of the term "swing the club." He came to the United States and taught his theory of swinging the clubhead to a number of great champions. His books on this phase of golf are among the most popular in golf instruction.

Writing on the mental side of the game, Jones said, "The greatest obstacle to learning the golf swing is the mind. The conscious mind always interferes with the subconscious.

"Conscious effort to control the movement of the clubhead handicaps the expert as well as the duffer. When the expert permits his mind to interfere with his golf, it is said he didn't concentrate.

"In short, good golf must be played largely through subconscious control."

Jones' statement substantiates the theory that self-hypnosis is the aid to better golf. It is by reducing the distractions of the conscious mind and concentrating its attention upon a single object or thought that allows the stroke to be controlled by the subconscious mind.

In his instruction to acquire subconscious control, Jones writes: "Through constant repetition . . . practice . . . you must develop a muscular routine which makes correct stroking a habit. Once this is subconsciously controlled, you can repeat the effort whenever necessary without giving conscious thought as to how it is done."

Jones has described the subconscious feel, but the psychologists disagree with his theory as to how it is acquired. They point out that the mind cannot be trained through physical activity. Rather, it is the mind that trains the muscles during practice.

Stated more simply, the muscles are controlled by the nerves. The nerves receive their direction from the mind. This, then, places the control and training for physical activity in the mind.

Therefore, if you want to train your muscles, the first step you must take is to train that portion of the mind that controls them. In the golf stroke, it is the subconscious mind. The only means of direct contact with the subconscious mind is through hypnosis.

Dow Finsterwald, known to his fellow pros as "Down the Middle Dow," in discussing his game, said, "In answer to the question, 'What do you try to do on the backswing,' I have few sensations when playing. I try to be as automatic as possible."

Subconscious control is often described as "being automatic." Sensations or messages from the senses are received by the conscious mind. A lack of sensation indicates the stroke has been played subconsciously.

Of all the professionals, the one whom the spectators may see most obviously withdraw into his subconscious during play is Ben Hogan. Ed Furgol, commenting on Hogan's power of concentration, said: "Ben goes into the isolation booth the minute he saunters over to the practice tee. He doesn't come out of it until thirty minutes after he has finished a round."

This withdrawal into his subconscious, which is a complete limiting of the conscious mind to the point that he is almost completely unaware of the spectators, has won Hogan many championships.

Ben Hogan claims, "The average golfer is entirely

capable of building a repeating swing and breaking 80 if he learns to perform a small number of correct movements and, conversely, eliminates a lot of movements which tend to keep the swing from repeating."

It is the "lot of movements which tend to keep the swing from repeating" statement with which self-hypnosis is concerned.

Psychologists have determined these unwanted muscle movements are created by tension which is caused by a fear in the conscious mind.

For proof you need only ask yourself what causes you to jump and your body to become rigid when there is an unexpected, loud noise. It is muscle tension that causes you to say, "I was scared stiff." It is fear-producing tension which causes a golfer to freeze on a shot.

Gene Sarazen, in writing on putting, made note of fear which produces muscle tension when he said: "As every senior well knows, the first part of your game to deteriorate, as you advance in years, is your putting stroke. It's a curious thing how it leaves you. It happens first on the short putts, and then on the longer ones.

"When you pass forty-five, your thinking is governed by fear. You are aways allowing for errors. When you are older, you know all the ways a putt can be missed. The youngsters, however, only see the hole."

What you have read so far can be likened to shouting instructions to a drowning man that the way to keep from drowning is to swim. Unless he previously had swimming instruction the advice is of little value. You have been told by the experts what you should do. Now, you will learn how to do it.

Chapter 4

WHAT YOU SHOULD KNOW ABOUT
SELF-HYPNOSIS

The induction of self-hypnosis is easy once you understand the relationship between the conscious and subconscious mind.

Think of your mind as two separate parts with a wall between them. This wall keeps all information received by the conscious mind from reaching the subconscious mind until it has been screened through experience, knowledge, and logic. During hypnosis, this wall is removed.

The subconscious mind is the "old mind," and man shares it with all other living creatures. It has no reasoning power, only instinct. The conscious mind is called the "new mind," or the "mind of man." It is this new mind, with the power to reason, that makes man superior to all creatures on earth. Other creatures act through instinct.

Even trained animals perform only through conditioning, fear, hunger, or a need for security. However, man, if he wishes, may use his conscious mind to direct his actions by logic.

The conscious mind receives all messages directed to the brain from the senses. It receives pictures through the eyes, sound through the ears, pain from the nerves, and so forth.

It is equipped with a filtering system that analyzes every report it receives. It judges the truth of the reports by testing them against experience and knowledge. Then it analyzes them with logic. After the report has been judged, it is given to the subconscious mind to be permanently recorded.

The subconscious mind has no filtering system. It accepts everything it receives as truth and records it as fact. Because the subconscious mind has no power to reason and accepts everything given it as truth, it cannot alter any message it receives.

Right now, if you were told you would have no sensation of pain if you placed the lighted end of a cigarette against the back of your hand, you wouldn't do it. Why not? Because this message was filtered by reason in your conscious mind and held to be false. You knew from past experience that the lighted end of a cigarette would burn you.

However, if you were under hypnosis, the message would have bypassed your conscious mind and would have gone directly to your subconscious. Therefore, the statement could not have been challenged through experience, knowledge, or logic, and you would feel no pain if such a suggestion were given.

"But," you ask, "if the cigarette were held against my hand long enough, wouldn't it have burned the flesh even though I felt no pain?"

Yes, it most certainly would have created a burn. Hypnosis is not contrary to any physical law.

Hindu fakirs use this knowledge to perform their hot coals trick. Their feet are calloused to keep the flesh from burning, but the intense heat would still cause them extreme pain if they were not under hypnosis. Hypnosis amounts to pulling the off-switch to the higher nerve centers that transmit pain.

Much of the misconception concerning hypnosis arises from the idea that it is possible to use hypnosis contrary to physical law. When such a phenomenon occurs, it is an hallucination.

If you were hypnotized, a hypnotist might hand you a lemon and tell you it was candy. If you tasted it, you would find it sweet, because your subconscious mind accepted his suggestion as true. However, he did not turn the lemon into candy. He only created an hallucination in your subconscious mind.

Would it be an hallucination if you told yourself, while under self-hypnosis, that you were going to be a better golfer?

It might be, if that was the only direction you gave to your subconscious mind.

If you were hypnotized by a professional player who could give your subconscious mind muscle direction, he might cause you to play a fairly good game, but only when you know the physical movements necessary to hit a golf ball can self-hypnosis improve your game permanently.

Golf professionals hit the ball with an automatic swing. What they are actually doing is using their subconscious mind to make the stroke. When you let your conscious mind with its reasoning power control the action, you are aware of all the penalties involved. This creates fear which, in turn, produces muscle tension.

How can you tell whether it is your conscious or subconscious mind that is being used when you make the shot? Very easily. If you feel any strain, any sensation of muscle tautness or tension, you can be sure your conscious mind is directing the stroke. The subconscious mind, because its actions are automatic, lacks sensation in the usual meaning of the word.

This is called the subconscious feel and may be tested as follows: Write your name on a piece of paper and note how you feel (or lack feel) as you do it. Now, try to consciously copy it and note the muscle strain produced from the conscious mind.

The subconscious feel is the rhythm you have during a practice swing, or that "sweet feeling" when a stroke is played right. Any conscious effort produces muscle tension. This is what is meant when you are told "you are trying too hard." Your conscious mind is so concerned with the mechanical movements and your desire to hit the ball that it produces muscle tension. It is what golfers call "freezing" on a shot.

WHAT YOU SHOULD KNOW ABOUT SELF-HYPNOSIS

As you know, one of the most obvious flaws of the high-handicap player is a tightening or tension in the right forearm at the start of the backswing. This action is caused by the conscious mind calling upon its "trusty right hand" to assist with the shot. It makes it impossible to keep the right elbow down and the right arm folded into the body during the stroke. If the right elbow points out instead of down as it should, the right shoulder cannot be brought in low. This results in an outside-in swing.

What, then, do you do with your conscious mind when you play?

You do the same thing a hypnotist does. You fixate it on a single object, in this case upon the ball. The physical act of hypnosis is fixating the attention of the conscious mind upon an object or thought to distract it from other thoughts so that contact may be made with the subconscious mind. This is what a hypnotist does when he uses a disk or some other object to focus the conscious attention of a subject.

In hypnosis, the attention is fixed. The next time you're out on the course and stand up to make your swing, note how your conscious mind gives a little attention to all your sense organs. As you stand there, you see a little, you hear a little, you feel a little. You are conscious of many things going on around you, but your attention is not fixed on any one particular thing. Hypnosis shuts off conscious distractions, and lets you concentrate. The results are miraculous.

The importance of fixating the conscious mind while executing the golf stroke may be observed in a statement made by Julius Boros, after he won the U. S. Open title in 1952. "I knew I won it because I didn't choke up," he said. "Before I started, I told myself I would have to play every shot quickly, because I knew if I dallied too long, I would start thinking of the consequences and if I tensed up . . . that would have finished it."

Boros created a state of self-hypnosis by deliberately not allowing his conscious mind to dwell on the consequences. Tension is produced when the conscious mind is aware that a penalty is involved in an action.

To fully understand self-hypnosis you should have a clear picture of the nature of conditioned reflexes. A conditioned reflex may be defined as a psychological or physiological response to a specific stimulus, resulting from training or experience. When it is established by repetition, these responses then become involuntary.

The goal in learning self-hypnosis is to establish a conditioned reflex to a specific stimulus. This is done by repeatedly "feeding yourself" stimuli that produce hypnosis.

Each time you practice self-hypnosis you should give yourself the post-hypnotic suggestion that the next time you want to hypnotize yourself, all you have to do is relax, count to three, and you will fall into the state of hypnosis necessary for your purpose. This stimulus (post-hypnotic command) produces the conditioned reflex (hypnosis). The key words (one, two, three) become associated with the action that you seek. By repetition, just thinking about the stimulus can bring on the response. This is what happens on the golf course when the subconscious feel is brought into play. By using self-hypnosis on the fairways, you can call upon the subconscious feel at any time to help you make a certain shot.

You must form the habit of being able to go into the hypnotic state wherever and whenever you want. Habits control you automatically, whether you recognize their effects or not. They are essential to life, and without them nothing could be accomplished.

Imagine the dilemma you would be in if you had to relearn how to handle a car every time you drove. When you were learning to drive, you had to remember a number of little things in order to start the motor — to shift into gear to get rolling, to handle the car on the road, and to park and stop it when you got to your destination. After practicing the routine of driving for awhile, you formed the necessary habits so that most of the procedures became automatic. Now, when you drive, the stimulus of getting into your car activates the conditioned reflexes needed for driving. Once you had formed the correct habits your subconscious mind took over the major part of driving: starting, steering, braking, stopping, parking.

Typing is another example of conditioned reflexes at work. In the beginning a typist learns the placement of the letters on the keyboard with difficulty. Her speed is slow, and she has to think every time her finger touches a key. However, once the habit of typing is instilled in her subconscious mind, it becomes automatic, and she types with no conscious thought or effort.

When you form habits you are painfully conscious, at first, of every move you make. When they start to become automatic, you know the subconscious is taking over more and more of the work. It is well to keep in mind that success in self-hypnosis depends largely upon setting up such an habitual stimulus-response cycle that the desired self-hypnotic state is easily induced.

It is impossible for anyone to state how much time this conditioning will require, since so much depends upon your sincerity and application. But conditioned reflexes can be achieved by anyone who is sufficiently conscientious and interested.

It is foolish, however, to learn any technique of action unless your goal is well thought out. You can create in yourself new conditioned reflexes, but you should understand just what you want to do with them. You should have a very clear picture of the ideal golfer that you want to be. Whatever originates in your conscious mind must be controlled before you send it on to your subconscious because once there it works automatically. This necessitates careful analysis before a session of self-hypnosis. Should you give your subconscious mind wrong directions on how to handle your club in a certain shot, you're going to be disappointed in your score the next time you play. Be certain that the directions you give yourself while under hypnosis are the correct ones. Train yourself on the driving range until the correct stance, grip, and swing become habitual. Then, when you practice them under hypnosis using visual imagery, the subconscious feel will be right and will work for you.

You must understand that your subconscious mind is fully capable of making a golf shot. Don't you trust it when you walk, eat, drive a car, and do innumerable other things without conscious effort? If you give it the correct directions, it can be trusted much more than your conscious mind, because it has no power to reason and cannot change any message or direction.

Remember, it takes time to form a new habit. Think how many years it took you to learn to read and write. You were often discouraged. Yet this knowledge is invaluable to you now. When it comes to establishing a conditioned reflex in self-hypnosis, a few of you will forget that learning comes from repetition and will want success in an hour. You will only achieve success when you realize that it will take time. You should work every day at forming the habit of self-hypnosis. If you do, you cannot help but succeed in establishing the subconscious feel that is necessary in good golf playing.

Chapter 5

HOW TO ACHIEVE SELF-HYPNOSIS

Hypnosis, as stated, is a recognized phenomenon. If you accept this statement, you have met the only requirement necessary to induce hypnosis.

A comfortable chair, a quiet and not-too-brightly lighted room, and the assurance of being undisturbed is all that is needed for the environment. Actually, you will find being in bed most satisfactory. It has the added advantage that at the completion of self-hypnosis you can drop right off to sleep.

Don't be afraid of inducing self-hypnosis. As Dr. Dorcus stated, "A hypnotized person won't do anything unless he wants to and won't stay in a trance if he wants to come out of it." The feeling you have as you enter the first stage of hypnosis may be compared to the moment before you drop off to sleep. If you wished, by sheer will power, you could rouse yourself and refuse to sleep. We are assuming, of course, that you really wish to be hypnotized.

The directions you give yourself need not be spoken aloud nor need they be given by rote. The words used in the following instructions are given only as one example of how to induce self-hypnosis. You should use words that are familiar to you and give yourself suggestions that will help your individual game.

Induce self-hypnosis as follows: Turn the lights out, lie down in a comfortable position on the bed and close your eyes. Say to yourself:

"I am now going to relax every muscle in my body . . . starting from my feet . . . and going to my head . . . The toes on my right foot are relaxing . . . They feel limp . . . limp . . . heavy and relaxed . . . This relaxation is creeping up through the ball and the arch of my foot . . . all the way to my ankle . . . so that my right foot is completely relaxed . . . relaxed and heavy . . . heavy and limp . . . Now the toes on my left foot are relaxing in the same way . . . First my toes . . . limp and heavy . . . Now my left arch and heel . . . heavy and relaxed . . . heavy and limp . . . My left foot is completely relaxed . . . relaxed and limp . . . My left foot is completely relaxed . . . Both feet are now completely relaxed . . . completely relaxed . . . relaxed and heavy . . . This heaviness is creeping up the calf of my right leg . . . so that I am now completely relaxed from the tip of my right toes to my knee . . . Now my left calf is relaxing in the same manner . . . Both of my feet and legs are completely relaxed up to my knees

... This relaxation is extending up through the large muscles of my right thigh ... so that my right leg is completely relaxed up to my hip ... Now I am letting my left thigh also relax ... so that both of my feet and legs are heavy ... heavy and relaxed ... heavy and relaxed ... relaxed and limp ... so relaxed ... so limp ... Now the fingers on my right hand are relaxing ... They are getting limp and heavy ... and relaxed ... I feel my right hand relaxing more and more ... getting more and more limp ... more and more heavy ... Now the fingers of my left hand are letting go completely ... All the muscles are relaxing ... My fingers are getting heavy ... limp ... relaxed ... My left hand is now completely relaxed and heavy ... This feeling is now flowing up my arms ... My right forearm is relaxed and heavy ... My left forearm limp and heavy ... My right upper arm is relaxed ... heavy ... heavy ... My left upper arm is relaxed ... relaxed and limp ... Both of my hands and arms are completely relaxed ... relaxed and heavy ... heavy and limp ... Now I am going to relax my body ... My hips ... back muscles ... abdomen ... chest muscles ... shoulders ... will all relax at the same time ... I shall take a deep breath ... hold it ... and release it slowly ... My entire body is relaxing ... I am breathing deeply ... and slowly ... My body is now completely relaxed ... I feel pleasantly limp and heavy ... relaxed and limp ... My body is completely relaxed ... and I am breathing slowly ... evenly ... The muscles in my neck are now beginning to relax ... My head is becoming so heavy ... All the muscles in my face are limp ... relaxed and loose ... From

my neck to the top of my head I am completely relaxed
... I feel pleasantly free from tension ... Every muscle
and every nerve in my entire body is completely relaxed
... My body feels loose ... and heavy ... completely relaxed ... My body is resting calmly ... I am fully at ease
... Every muscle ... every nerve ... in my entire body
... is completely relaxed ..."

It is very important to relax your body thoroughly
before continuing with self-hypnosis. Should you have
trouble relaxing any part of your body, you can make it
release all its tension by concentrating upon it individ-
ually. After each instruction you give yourself, be sure to
pause until it works. Do not will your body to relax. This
only brings the conscious mind into play and defeats
your purpose. When you have attained this feeling of
relaxation over your entire body, open your eyes.

Select an object above eye level, so that there is a slight
strain on the eyes and eyelids. A bit of light reflection, a
picture frame, or where the wall joins the ceiling does
nicely for a focal point. At this time you try to get your
eyelids to close at a specific count such as the count of
three. This could just as well be a count of ten, twenty,
or one hundred. Actually you are trying to establish a
conditioned response to a specific count. When you have
an irresistible urge to close your eyes on or before you
reach the completion of the count, you know that you are
in a heightened state of suggestibility or self-hypnosis.
This is the first test for determining if you have achieved
self-hypnosis. You do not rush the count, but try to consciously create a heavy, watery feeling which you again

purposely intensify by self-suggestion as you continue counting until such time that you close your eyes because it becomes uncomfortable to keep them open. You may accomplish this readily or it may take you five, ten, or fifteen minutes. Whatever time is necessary initially to accomplish this will be decreased as you condition yourself every night.

Let us suppose that you try to get an eye closure but the test doesn't work. You either are not taking enough time to first relax, you are not in the right psychological frame of mind or the conditioning process hasn't yet been established sufficiently. If this is the case, take more time to achieve a good state of relaxation and adopt the attitude that you are entering into a very beneficial and pleasurable state. Lastly, if your eyes do not close involuntarily, close them voluntarily and follow through with the desired post-hypnotic suggestions *as though you were in the hypnotic state.* The last statement is very important because as you do this, the conditioned response pattern will be established and you will achieve the positive results that you desire.

Here are suggestions that you can use to accomplish the eye test. Remember, do not memorize the exact words; just the form is important. The following suggestions should be correlated with your psychological as well as physical reactions:

"As I complete the count of ten, my eyelids will become very heavy, watery, and tired. Even before I complete the count of ten, it may become necessary for me to close my eyes. The moment I do, I shall fall into a state of self-hypnosis. I shall be fully conscious, hear everything, and be able to direct suggestions to my subconscious mind. *One* . . . my eyelids are becoming very heavy . . . *Two* . . . My eyelids are becoming very watery . . . *Three* . . . My eyelids are becoming very tired . . . *Four* . . . I can hardly keep my eyes open . . . *Five* . . . I am beginning to close my eyes . . . *Six* . . . My eyelids are closing more and more . . . *Seven* . . . I am completely relaxed and at ease . . . *Eight* . . . It is becoming impossible for me to keep my eyelids open . . . *Nine* . . . It is impossible for me to keep my eyelids open . . . *Ten* . . . My eyes are closed, I am in the self-hypnotic state, and I can give myself whatever post-hypnotic suggestions I desire."

At this point, using the visual imagery technique, you mentally picture the good golfer that you want to be. You visualize yourself playing with perfect form and in an easy and relaxed manner. You might feel a bit uneasy about giving yourself these suggestions, but do it! It's your key to better golf.

Here is another test you can use to determine if you have achieved self-hypnosis. You can give yourself this test directly after your period of relaxation or following the eye closure test. This test is known as the swallowing test. Here are the suggestions you can use:

"As I count to ten and even before I reach the count of ten, I shall get an irresistable urge to swallow one time. As soon as I swallow one time, this feeling will leave me and I'll feel normal again in every respect. *One* . . . My lips are dry . . . *Two* . . My throat is becoming dry . . . *Three* . . . I am beginning to get an urge to swallow . . .

Four . . . This urge is becoming stronger . . . *Five* . . . My throat feels parched . . . *Six* . . . The urge to swallow is becoming stronger and stronger . . . *Seven* . . . I feel an involuntary urge to swallow . . . *Eight* . . . This involuntary urge is becoming stronger and stronger . . . *Nine* . . . I must swallow . . . *Ten* . . . I have swallowed one time and am now in a self-hypnotic state in which I am very receptive to positive suggestions."

With this test you wait until you swallow without conscious direction. When you do, you know you have achieved a state of heightened suggestibility. The act of swallowing has been directed and controlled by your subconscious mind as ordered by your conscious mind. After the swallowing test is successfully completed, you can give yourself whatever suggestions you want pertaining to your golf game.

Here is a third test you can use for determining your receptivity to suggestions. You use the same general pattern that you did for the eye closure test and swallowing test. Remember, these suggestions should not be memorized verbatim; just the form is important.

"As I count ten and even before I reach the count of ten, I shall experience a tingling, light, or numb feeling in my right hand . . . *One* . . . I am concentrating upon my right hand . . . As I think of it, picture it . . . completely relaxed . . . *Two* . . . I shall feel a pleasant . . . tingling . . . sensation . . . in my hand . . . *Three* . . . In my mind . . . I see my right hand . . . It is limp . . . and heavy . . . very relaxed . . . *Four* . . . I am completely at ease . . . *Five* . . . My hand is beginning to tingle . . . *Six* . . . It is a very

pleasant sensation . . . relaxed . . . tingling . . . *Seven* . . .
It is becoming stronger and stronger . . . *Eight* . . . It is a
very pleasant feeling . . . *Nine* . . . I can feel a very pleasant, tingling feeling . . . *Ten* . . . I am now in a state of
self-hypnosis and can give myself beneficial post-hypnotic
suggestion especially pertaining to playing a better game
of golf . . ."

If your subconscious mind has taken over, you will find
your right hand has a tingling sensation in it. *You must
remember* after any test with body action, a direction
must be given to have it return to normal. Otherwise, the
light, tingling sensation could continue after the completion of hypnosis. Now you say:

"The sensation in my hand will go away; it will return
to normal . . . I now have proof . . . that I have reached a
state of hypnosis . . . Every muscle . . . and nerve . . . in my
entire body . . . is completely relaxed . . . I feel wonderfully well . . . I shall now give constructive instructions to
my subconscious mind . . . in order to improve my golf
game . . ."

At this point, you may start giving yourself specific
suggestions for improving your golf game. These suggestions should be carefully planned in advance of induction
so you will know what to tell your subconscious mind at
this point. Give the mental pictures and suggestions to
yourself positively so as to remove the need for examination or challenge by your conscious mind. All you are
seeking to do in self-hypnosis is to distract your conscious
mind, thus eliminating the power of reasoning.

Picture yourself in the place of a professional or good

golfer you know, making the golf swing as you have studied it. Repeat the swing using a visual image until there is a subconscious "feel" that it could not be made in any other way. Remember, it is this subconscious feel that is being sought so that it may be activated during actual play.

Too much cannot be said concerning the subconscious feel. You will know what it is to have confidence in your game once you receive it. You will be able to play golf without stress or strain. Unless the subconscious feel has been deeply implanted so that the subconscious mind can play the stroke automatically, distracting the conscious mind is useless.

Once you have received the sensation of the subconscious feel, even if it lasts only a few strokes in practice or a few strokes during a round, you will realize how important it is to reactivate it in order to attain the automatic swing.

Any directions given to the subconscious mind will be carried out unless countermanded during hypnosis. These directions are known as post-hypnotic suggestions which you give to yourself to be executed after you have terminated the hypnotic state. They may be effective for months and even years after the original post-hypnotic suggestion was given.

When you have finished implanting suggestions for better golf in your subconscious mind, you should give yourself a post-hypnotic suggestion that the next time you practice self-hypnosis you will enter a deeper state more quickly. This is the technique used by hypnotists to facilitate hypnosis in the same subject the next time. Say to yourself:

"The next time I hypnotize myself . . . I shall fall into a deeper . . . and more relaxed state . . . I will be able to relax my body more quickly . . . and easily . . . The next time I play golf . . . my body will be relaxed . . . and my mind will be at ease . . . The subconscious feel I have just experienced . . . will be brought into play . . . and my game will improve . . . I know these positive suggestions will work for me . . . At the count of three . . . I will open my eyes . . . I will be completely relaxed . . . and at ease . . . At the count of three . . . I will feel wonderfully refreshed . . . I will feel wide awake . . . and full of renewed energy . . . At the count of three . . . I will open my eyes . . . and feel completely relaxed . . . *One* . . . Every muscle . . . every nerve . . . in my entire body is completely relaxed . . . I feel wonderfully relaxed . . . *Two* . . . Every muscle . . . every nerve . . . in my entire body is relaxed . . . and rested . . . I feel wonderfully well . . . completely relaxed . . . *Three* . . . My eyes are open . . . and I feel wonderfully refreshed . . . completely relaxed . . ."

The three tests you have been given for proof of self-hypnosis are sufficient. Additional tests are not needed. You will find that after you have practiced self-hypnosis for a short period these tests will no longer be necessary because you will recognize instantly when you are in a hypnotic state.

You must remember that even though you feel you may not have achieved hypnosis (which is common), the suggestions you give yourself must, of necessity, spill over into your subconscious mind. This means the suggestions will work for you even though you do not feel as you anticipated.

Why is it so difficult to believe you are in a hypnotic state? Because you do not feel any appreciable difference from your normal waking state. You are probably looking for something to happen. Since you don't know what this "something" is, you are positive you are not hypnotized because you are aware of everything that is going on. You are not knocked out, and, because of this, you reason you are not under hypnosis.

The easiest way to recognize if you have reached the hypnotic state is to give yourself the three tests: eye closure, swallowing, and hand tingling. If you achieve only one of these tests, the others will come through practice. If you achieve none, then take a longer count. You can count to 100 if you need this period of time to assure eye closure. The closing of the eyes is the first sign that you are in a receptive frame of mind. Regardless of the depth that you have achieved, and whether or not you have responded to any of the tests, *you should always give yourself whatever suggestions you desire as though you were in a very deep state of hypnosis.* "But," you ask, "if I'm not under hypnosis, why give myself the suggestions?" You do this so that you will begin to form the conditioned reflex pattern.

Should you fall asleep while working with self-hypnosis, it is perfectly all right. The suggestions will reach the subconscious while you are passing from consciousness to sleep.

BETTER GOLF USING SELF-HYPNOSIS

Some of you will achieve self-hypnosis almost instantaneously; others will succeed only after many weeks of practice. The important point to keep in mind is that if you persevere you will finally acquire the conditioned reflex pattern which is the basis of self-hypnosis. Keep at it.

Chapter 6

BETTER GOLF THROUGH MENTAL PICTURES

The secret of good golf is the employment of the visual image or mental picture.

There are two mental pictures used to improve golf. One is the visual image of the swing; the other is the flight of the ball.

You must get into your mind a clear picture of what your clubs and body ought to do during a stroke. Picture your favorite pro making a perfect swing. You will notice its main characteristics are power, rhythm, and balance. Once you have it fixed firmly in your mind, try to model your own swing after it. Instead of seeing the professional make the swing, picture yourself doing it. Make it so real in your mind that you actually feel the swing of the club and see the flight of the ball.

Horton Smith, who collected 33 titles during his career,

suggests: "Try to develop a mental picture of the ideal swing, whether it be that of a single player, or a composite of the features of several. I visualize a composite of such players as Chick Evans, Walter Hagen, and Bobby Jones and try to blend them into a personalized swing of my own."

Lloyd Mangrum, in his book, *Golf . . . A New Approach,* reveals how he deliberately tried to copy the swing of Sam Snead, the short game of Johnny Revolta, and the putting style of Horton Smith.

Don't be afraid of following this advice just because someone has told you that every golfer swings differently. It isn't true! Bob Toski, known as "Mighty Mouse," stands 5'8" and weighs 127 pounds. Yet, he has the same basic movements in his golf swing as does George Bayer, former University of Washington football star tackle, who has a powerful 6'5½" frame and 260 pounds of solid muscle. He is one of the mightiest hitters in the game, once belting a tee shot seven yards past the flag on a 435-yard hole. What may appear to be a difference in swing is only individual peculiarities and temperament.

By using visual imagery, you see yourself in the champion's place. You are actually making the swing of the professional in your mental movie. It is this transference of identity that produces the subconscious feel. It is formed in your conscious mind by a combination of messages received from your senses. Details of the picture are moulded upon experience, knowledge and logic. Your conscious mind records this mental picture as feel in your subconscious mind.

The subconscious mind must be trained, educated, or, more correctly, given the thought pattern to execute its directions to the muscles. Have you ever noticed how a child walks haltingly, by conscious imitation, until the subconscious thought pattern has been established? Any new physical movement, from learning to walk to playing golf, is done slowly and without assurance until the movements have been committed to the subconscious feel.

For example, if you had to consciously think of the location of the letters on the keyboard of a typewriter, you would never become a proficient typist. If you were proficient, your conscious mind would only be concerned with the thoughts you wanted to express. No conscious effort would be given to spelling the words. Words and phrases, which might appear to be conscious thought, would be fed into the typewriter subconsciously.

This typing pattern is broken only when the subconscious mind has not received proper training. If the thought pattern for the location of the keys, spelling, words and phrases has not been correctly recorded in your subconscious, the action falters while your conscious mind applies reasoning to determine what is correct.

The same thing can be applied to golf. The inexperienced player, like the beginning typist, falters when he tries to recall the correct golf movements. The errors he makes are like those of the typist striking the wrong key. Errors in judgment or using the wrong club are like those in grammar or using the wrong phrase.

The combined effort of the conscious and subconscious

minds to produce a single effect has long been the subject of speculation by psychologists. They have learned that the conscious mind issues the orders to effect an end result, and the subconscious mind produces it.

For example, when you run, your subconscious mind controls your leg muscles and body balance. You do not require a mental picture of your legs in motion to activate the subconscious feel. You need only give the order to run to produce the end result of running.

You come to a ditch. The ditch must be jumped. You have never jumped this particular ditch before so there is no mental picture on file in your subconscious mind as to what muscle action is required to carry your body across it. Your conscious mind takes over and forms a picture of the width of the ditch. It evaluates from past experience what will be required. If there is no error, and you jump the ditch successfully, the picture will then be filed in your subconscious mind as feel. The next time you come to this ditch, you need only activate the feel by issuing the command to jump.

When you came upon this ditch the first time, you had to pause to allow your conscious mind to make its evaluation. The next time you approached it, your subconscious responded instantly and automatically.

The correct grip, stance and body movement to produce a hook does not require any more conscious thought than running. For the average player, however, it is like coming to the ditch for the first time. He must consciously evaluate the muscle directions. Until he can call upon the subconscious feel recorded in practice sessions, he finds it impossible to think "hook," "fade," or any other type of shot.

When you want a drink of water, you do not consciously direct your hand to reach for the cup, your fingers to grasp the handle, your arm to move the cup to your lips, or your throat to swallow. You merely direct the end result; the desire for a drink of water. All of the mechanical action necessary to accomplish the feat is directed by your subconscious. There is only the passive sensation of the subconscious feel. There is not the tension or muscle strain which is felt during the period when the action is being produced by the conscious mind.

Conscious mental pictures provide the answer to the instructions given by professionals when they advise you to think a certain type of shot. As Jimmy Demaret stated: "Simply make up your mind what you are going to attempt to do with a particular shot. Then, once the shot is projected in your mind's eye, play it with confidence."

Professionals are able to think a shot because they need only consciously order the end result. They have already recorded the subconscious feel during their practice sessions.

The correct mental image of the swing is recorded in your subconscious mind as feel. To produce the end result, a good swing, your conscious mind need only activate your subconscious mind.

Since you have fourteen clubs in your bag and there are a variety of types of shots and distances possible with each club, it must follow that a mental picture for each stroke required to play a complete round must be recorded in your subconscious mind.

This is the reason why practice is absolutely necessary. Practice is the recording session for your subconscious mind. During practice your conscious mind must evaluate the correct muscles to be used and the amount of energy to produce the desired distance.

When you are hypnotized you mentally picture yourself making the golf swing as you physically practiced it. You must recall how the club felt in your hands, the grip you used, the rhythm of the swing, the follow through of the club after it hit the ball.

The subconscious mind, without reasoning power, cannot alter any mental picture given to it. Unless there is conscious interference it will play back the subconscious feel exactly as it received it. Without conscious interference your stroke then becomes as automatic as walking, drinking from a cup or running.

Pete Zangrillo, instructor at the driving range in Darien, Connecticut, says: "Do your thinking on the golf range, not on the golf course. That is the soundest advice a driving range pro or any golf instructor can give. The trouble is too few people realize how practical it is."

Big Mike Souchak phrases it this way: "Golf should be fun. Don't louse it up by doing your thinking on the course. This phase of the game should be done in the practice area. The hitting should be done on the course itself."

All they are trying to tell you is that the stroke must be recorded as subconscious feel. It can then be called upon during play without using the reasoning power of your conscious mind to determine what muscle movement is needed.

It is your conscious mind that keeps golf from becoming completely automatic. Fear is created when you are aware a penalty is involved in the action. This fear may be anything from the ball landing in a ditch, or the loss of a stroke, to the possible loss of a championship. Fear produces the tensions which destroy the subconscious feel by conscious interference. Automatic action is lost when conscious, unwanted muscle action is brought into play.

James Bender, in his book, *Victory Over Fear,* states: "The body never acts, it only reacts. That is why the fearful person is tense. The negative ideas he concentrates on are translated into negative bodily reactions."

If you are afraid of being unable to make a certain shot, you create a mental picture of failure. This creates the tension, which assures the failure.

Conscious concern in any action creates tension. As stated before, it is described by golfers as freezing on a shot. It is an apt expression, for tension contracts the muscles in the player's hands, forearms, shoulders and hips, making it impossible to achieve the rhythm of the automatic swing.

Confidence is the only antidote for the poison of fear. You gain confidence when your conscious mind knows it can call upon the subconscious feel to produce the end result of a desired stroke.

Dick Mayer, Open and World Champion, says: "I cannot overemphasize the importance of confidence. If you approach your putt with doubts, these doubts will be translated into your judgment and the putting stroke. It then becomes pure luck if the ball drops in."

Try closing your eyes while making practice swings. Picture the stroke in your mind. By switching the emphasis from the ball to the swing of the club, you will be astounded at the shot results you can achieve. Professionals actually sense where their clubhead is traveling and what it is doing. You can, too.

Remember, you cannot will yourself to play better golf because your will is completely influenced by your imagination. This influence of visual imagery or mental pictures upon the will has long been known to psychologists. If this is not true, why is it that you have no trouble in walking on a plank when it is resting on the ground, but if the plank were stretched across space between two high buildings your will could not make you walk across it. You are stopped by your imagination which has formed a mental picture of you falling.

It is the realization of the influence of the mental picture upon the will which makes clear the statement of Lealand Gustavson, in his book, *Enjoy Your Golf,* when he said: "Try to form an exact mental picture of just how your ball must travel to drop into the hole. Permit the mental picture to guide your subconscious efforts. That is what is meant by 'touch' on the putting green."

A correct mental picture of the swing, transferred to subconscious feel through hypnosis, will provide you with confidence. This confidence then creates a mental picture of success for the shot.

Be certain that you have the correct mental picture of

the swing. It is the three inches before the club strikes the ball and the three inches after impact that determines the success or failure of the shot.

A good way to study championship form is through the use of free motion picture films available at most public and college libraries. If you do not have a 16mm projector, you can rent one for a small fee at many of the motion picture supply houses.

A partial list of films available without cost to individuals and groups is listed at the end of this chapter.

The only effective way to employ the power of the mental picture is by committing it to your subconscious mind during hypnosis. It is no longer a visual image in your subconscious, but is transformed into subconscious feel.

FREE MOTION PICTURE FILMS

PRESSURE GOLF — (Color, sound, 16mm)

House of Seagram, 1430 Peel Street, Montreal, Quebec, also Canadian Film Library, 111 N. Wabash Avenue, Chicago, Illinois

1959 Canadian Open won by Doug Ford at Islemere G & CC, Montreal, Quebec. Similar films of 1956-7-8 Canadian Open also available.

MILLER OPEN — (Color, sound, 16mm, 30 minutes)

Miller Brewing Co., Film Section, Sales Promotion and Publicity Department, Milwaukee 1, Wisconsin

Gene Littler's win of the 1959 Miller Open in Milwaukee. Similar films of victories by Dr. Cary Middlecoff, 1958; Ken Venturi, 1957; and Ed Furgol, 1956 also available.

ALL STAR GOLF
  Miller Brewing Co., Film Section, Sales Promotion and
  Publicity Department, Milwaukee 1, Wisconsin
    Films of the television series
TROUBLE-SHOOTING WITH PAUL HARNEY
  Miller Brewing Co., Film Section, Sales Promotion and
  Publicity Department, Milwaukee 1, Wisconsin
    Shows how to play hilly lies, sand shots, intentional
    hooks and slices.
FAMOUS FAIRWAYS — (Color, sound, 16mm, 30
  minutes)
    A. G. Spaulding & Bros., Inc., 161 Sixth Avenue,
    New York 13, N. Y.
      Includes play on Pine Valley, N. J.; Pinehurst,
      N. C.; Southampton, N. Y.; Oakmont, Pa.; Pebble
      Beach and Cypress Point, Calif., golf courses.
TRICKS AND STICKS — (Black and white, sound,
  16mm, 24 minutes)
    Chamberlin Metal Products Co., 2226-A Wabansia,
    Chicago 47, Ill.
      Trick shot artist Paul Han exhibits his famous
      "impossible" shots.

Chapter 7

THE CHAMPIONS' SIX-INCH DRIVE

Every action in the golf swing has only one objective: To strike the ball squarely with the center of the clubface on a line of flight to the hole.

Hitting with the center of the clubface not only assists with direction, but is a deciding factor in distance. Tests made with a camera capable of stopping action at 1/9,000th of a second revealed that a ball struck squarely in the center of the clubface carried up to 50 yards further than when the hit was on the toe or heel.

When the clubface is not square a spin is imparted to the ball, causing it to hook or slice. Then, both direction and distance are lost.

With this in mind, visualize an expert as he brings the clubhead along the line of flight for at least three inches before impact and three inches after the hit.

Many experts claim this "six-inch drive" can be stretched to a foot or more. The longer it is, the less room there is for error.

However, the human body is so constructed that the clubhead can only be held on the line of flight for a short distance. With the body (the head in particular) as the axis for the swing, the club must be taken back on a line inside the line of flight, and returned to impact on a line inside the line of flight.

It is the opinion of some experts that the misconception many high-handicap players have about bringing the clubhead to the line of flight has been fostered by an overemphasis on the "inside-out" and "outside-in" swings.

All movements prior to reaching the position for the six-inch drive are only preparations to get your body and hands in position. All movements following it are only proof as to whether or not it has been correctly executed.

Before entering a discussion on the various parts of the swing, here is a warning: Do not contort yourself into any particular position to emulate the professional form, except as a check-point.

The jerky, incomplete swing, so often seen in the stroke of inexperienced players, is the result of the individual being consciously aware of some single phase of the swing. He may be so concerned with a tip he has received that he disregards the swing as a whole.

The golf swing may be compared to a circle. It is the combination of as many small segments as you wish to make it. Each segment is of a relative value to all other segments. Neither the golf swing nor a circle are complete until they are continuous.

Another common error is to overemphasize instruction. A straight left arm becomes a stiff left arm. The steady head freezes the body. The hip turn is exaggerated into a lunging motion.

Visualizing the swing as a tilted wagon wheel, you can see that it must be made on the inside of the line of flight. In the golf swing, the wagon wheel is flattened on the bottom to permit the six-inch drive. In a true arc, there would be no room for error.

If the clubhead contacts the ball while coming from inside-out (without the flattened six-inch drive), a push results. Coming from the outside-in, it is a pull. Combined with a clubface that is not square, it is compounded by a hook or slice.

The best shot with which to practice the six-inch drive is the very short chip. Bring the clubhead in on the line of flight. Carry it through the ball. With the clubface square, it must go in a straight line. Johnny Revolta explains and describes this motion in detail in his book, *Short Cuts To Better Golf*. You should read it if you are seeking further instruction on the physical stroke.

Watching the champions, either in tournaments, on television, or in the free movies suggested in the previous chapter, you will notice a little ritual takes place ahead of each shot, no matter what club is being used.

The star comes up to a spot behind the ball to line up the shot. This is to determine where he wants it to land and what kind of a stroke is required to put it there. He is forming the mental picture of the flight of the ball.

Next, he comes to one side of the ball and takes a quarterswing. It has been suggested this practice swing is a nervous movement. What he is actually doing is activating the subconscious feel. He is giving a conscious reminder to his subconscious as to just how his hands, arms, shoulders, hips and feet are going to react during the critical six-inch drive.

If the tournament stars who practice or play almost every day in the week find this reminder necessary to activate the subconscious feel, it might be well if you emulated it.

Taking his stance, he begins the waggle. This movement is possibly the most discussed and least defined action in golf. It has been described variously as "a nervous peculiarity," "a last minute release of tension," and "a way of getting the body in motion."

All are partially correct. The waggle is a miniature preview of the shot to be played. Note how the star waggles for a long shot, with a suggestion of the power of the hit. As the same star nears the green, the waggle quickens for crisp iron play. The pace slows for a lazy, fluffy shot to hold a green over an obstacle.

There is one movement in the professional's waggle (if you have not previously been aware of it and copied it) that may well reduce your handicap immediately. It puts into play what is known as "the fly caster's wrists."

The expert places the clubhead behind the ball. He raises it an inch or two as he checks the line of flight. Then, he lowers it to ball level again. This movement is repeated from two or three times by some players to a dozen or more by others. The length of time is determined by how long it takes an individual to formulate the mental picture and activate the subconscious feel.

The motion to be aware of is the raising of the wrists (brought up and forward, hence, the term "fly caster's wrists") as the clubhead is lowered. Most high handicap players use the reverse motion. They lower or bend their wrists, raising the hands.

There are several reasons why it is important to have this movement performed correctly. It firms the left hand and straightens (not stiffens) the left arm. It produces a solid feeling from the clubhead to the left shoulder. This assists in starting the first movement of the backswing as a simultaneous movement of the hands, arms and shoulders.

The fly caster's wrists also help supinate the left hand. The word "supinate" and its opposite "pronate" are often found in golf instruction. Aside from the technical dictionary definition, supination for the golfer means to be certain the wrists do not "roll over" during the swing.

In other words, the back of the left hand is faced toward the hole at address. It remains in this vertical position throughout the swing and is never allowed to point skyward.

Some English players and early golf instructors advocated pronation. The clubhead was rolled open on the backswing and rolled closed on the downswing. It required precise timing. Supinating the left wrist removes this margin for error.

As the waggle is completed, note how the star as he

sets the clubhead behind the ball for the final time makes a little forward motion with his hands and body. This is the "forward-press." The body is turned to the right in the backswing. If the weight is already on the right foot or shifted there too quickly, it may produce a sway. Setting the weight to the left with the forward-press offsets this tendency.

Much of the cause for sway (pulling the body to the right of the ball) is caused by "picking up" the club with the right hand instead of starting the movement in one piece. The forward-press and fly caster's wrists help eliminate this error.

The head and spine are the axis for the swing. They must remain parallel to the ball throughout the swing. It is claimed some good players sway a little. This is setting up room for error. Unless the sway is brought back equal to that of the address position, the clubhead cannot contact the ball squarely.

There is one final movement in the waggle, more accurately described as the first movement of the take-away. The star, as he goes into the forward-press, flexes both knees. This produces a semi-sitting position. It keeps the knees flexible and the hips from locking throughout the swing.

With the knees straight or the hips locked, the body turn is restricted. When this takes place, instead of turning, the swing becomes an exaggerated sway.

There is considerable variation in grips. Some use the inter-lock, others the over-lap (known as the Vardon grip), while the baseball (ten finger grip) has been made popular by Art Wall, Bob Rosburg and Johnny Revolta. The "V's" between the thumbs and forefingers may point anywhere from the chin to the right shoulder.

In the grip, there are two points of universal agreement. One, the shaft is held in the palm and fingers of the left hand. Two, it is held only in the fingers of the right hand. Any variation causes trouble.

Many high handicap players put the grip too much in the right hand, thinking they can steer the shot. This results in an outside-in swing, with a resulting slice.

A serious flaw in the grip is often caused by a pincer movement between the thumb and forefinger of the right hand. It activates the muscles of the right forearm, making it impossible to fold the right arm in close to the body during the swing. Unless the right elbow is pointed down, the swing cannot be made without moving the axis or producing a sway.

Now, pick up a club and take your stance for the drive, with your feet about as far apart as the width of your shoulders. Your feet are brought closer together and your left foot withdrawn from the line of flight as the short irons are used.

Place the clubhead behind the ball. There is almost a straight line from the clubhead to your right shoulder. Now, if your arms are the same length, your right hand cannot reach below your left hand unless something "gives."

What gives is your right knee. Flex it and turn it slightly toward the ball. This lowers your right hip, which is turned ever so slightly toward the ball. Your right shoulder is lowered.

In the correct position you should have a sensation of looking down the fairway instead of at a right angle to the ball. You should have the feeling that the clubhead can be taken away and returned on the line of flight to produce the champions' six-inch drive.

If this sequence is not followed, your right shoulder will be pushed out so that your right hand can reach below your left hand. The take-away and return will then be on a line outside the line of flight. This thrust-out right shoulder is often termed the "natural slice" position.

The act of dropping the right shoulder has been called an occupational hazard for golfers. Note how many of them stand in this lopsided position, even without a club in their hands.

The take-away is started altogether by simultaneously turning your shoulders, arms and hands. It is the most critical movement in the golf swing. Should your hands or arms lead your shoulders, your arms will cross your chest and cause a locked position before the swing is completed. Your left shoulder cannot be brought under your chin.

Check this often. Unless your left shoulder comes under your chin, the full power of the golf swing cannot be generated. Further, the club cannot be brought back on a line inside the line of flight. The clubhead cannot reach the position for the six-inch drive.

As your shoulders turn, your hips are forced to turn. Your left knee points toward the ball. The term "hip turn" is often misleading. It is a withdrawal of the right hip rather than a circular motion. Check to see how the professional golfer withdraws his right hip almost straight back at a right angle from the line of the flight of the ball.

At the top of the backswing, with your right elbow down, your right hip withdrawn and your hands gripping the club so that the face is still squared, there is only one movement to be made to start the downswing. In fact, it is the only movement you can make if the hit is to be successful. It is the withdrawal of your left hip. This leaves a path for your hands and arms to come in close to your body and brings the clubhead along the line of flight.

The downswing must be made with no other movement than the withdrawal of your left hip. Starting it with your hands, arms, or shoulders will throw the clubhead on a line outside the line of flight.

Keep in mind that the backswing is initiated by the upper half of your body; the downswing is initiated by the lower half.

Your right hip returns only to a line parallel to the address position. If it goes beyond this it will cause the outside-in swing. Your right shoulder comes down, and this effects the flattened bottom of the wagon-wheel swing so that the clubhead can be brought along the line of flight.

The experts advise a pause at the top of the backswing to assist the player in making the first movement of the downswing with the hips.

Tommy Armour says: "I play with a lot of golfers who

score around 100, and each time I start out with one I reconcile myself to seeing at least ten strokes wasted by jerky swings. The pity is that this fault can be avoided by attention to one simple thing — that slight pause at the top of the backswing."

Jackie Burke says: "On any golf shot, once you have addressed the ball properly, the most important single act you can perform is to pause between your backswing and your downswing."

This advice, to pause at the top, is the essence of the instruction for a slow backswing. A golfer cannot change his temperament by putting on a pair of spiked shoes. If he is normally quick, he will spoil his timing by deliberately slowing down. The pause at the top is all that is necessary.

Among professional players, Dr. Cary Middlecoff has the most pronounced pause at the top of his backswing. In an interview, he explained: "It seems to give me time to get the hips moving and to be sure everything is all right before I start the downswing."

You may try this experiment in your living room for proof. Set a pillow against the wall as a backstop for the ball. Then, place a book on end on the carpet. Try chipping over the book with a seven or eight iron. Unless the clubface is brought in on the line of flight, with the clubface squared, the ball will not hop over the book. See how much easier it is to line up the clubface and bring it in for the champions' six-inch drive by a slight pause before the downswing.

Have you heard the common comment that "only tall,

skinny people can handle an upright swing"? Chubby "Porky" Oliver answers this with: "The difference between the baseball swing and the upright or vertical swing should come in for attention because no one ever can become an accomplished golfer if he insists on hitting with a swing that is horizontal."

With the horizontal or flat backswing it is impossible to flatten the bottom of the wagon wheel for the six-inch drive. Unless the timing is perfect for the flat backswing, and contact with the ball is being made at the exact instant the swing changes from inside to outside, the ball cannot be driven straight.

Discussion of the various mechanical movements could, and often does, go on for a 100 or more pages in golf instruction books. However, seeing the correct action in sequence pictures or motion pictures of the champions is all you need to form your mental movie upon which you may pattern your own swing during hypnosis.

"But," you ask, "how can I possibly remember all these movements during the two seconds it takes to make a golf swing?"

You can remember them all!

Not only will you be able to remember them all, but you will be able to execute them in the exact sequence for the perfect golf stroke in the two seconds required for the swing. Self-hypnosis is the answer.

Chapter 8

SEVEN HOURS PRACTICE IN SEVEN MINUTES

The subconscious mind does not record the passage of time the same way as the conscious mind.

The conscious mind records time physically, by means of a clock. It is objective and tells you that a thought or movement requires a certain number of seconds, minutes, hours, or days.

Your subconscious mind has an entirely different concept of time that has nothing to do with the physical world. It is called subjective because your own sense of the passage of time is used.

Personal time varies according to the circumstances in which you find yourself. Haven't you noticed that when you are happy or extremely interested in something, time

89

passes quickly? On the other hand, if you are sad or anxious, time seems to drag.

This is called time distortion. When you continue in a happy state, time is automatically shortened. When you are in a state of unhappiness, pain or anxiety, time automatically lengthens. This explains why a drowning man can review his entire life within seconds. Psychologists know this is possible, because your subconscious mind contains a complete record of everything that has happened to you since birth. Therefore, in moments of extreme distress your subconscious has the ability to distort and manipulate time.

If you have ever encountered danger or had a narrow escape, you probably experienced time distortion. Everything about you went into slow motion, and time seemed to stand still until the action was over. At that point, objective time started up again and everything returned to normal.

Have you ever heard someone say that it always seems shorter on the way back than it does going? The reason for this is that on the way to a place the conscious mind is alert to directions. On the way back, the subconscious knows the way and the conscious mind is occupied with other things. Therefore, subjectively speaking, the time involved in returning would seem shorter. Albert Einstein said that subjective time is not measurable.

Another example of time distortion happens when you dream. A dream which seemingly goes on for hours is actually experienced in a few seconds or minutes by the clock.

The theory of "sleep learning" is derived from this fact. Ramon Vinay, the talented Metropolitan opera star, used it to great advantage when he accepted a role to sing opposite Kirsten Flagstad in *Tristan*. Being unavoidably detained in Chile, he was unable to reach San Francisco in time for rehearsals. He memorized his role by sleeping with the speaker of an automatic record player under his pillow. The music was imbued so well in his subconscious mind that he was able to sing the role in a language he did not understand without missing a single cue. With only two piano rehearsals and one rehearsal with the orchestra, he sang so well that opera critic Alfred Frankenstein wrote: "He brought a tenderness, lyricism and fragility of expression that were altogether unprecedented."

Time sense can be deliberately altered by hypnotic suggestion. Employing time distortion under hypnosis, it is possible to imbue the subconscious mind with thought patterns in an inconceivably short period. Thus, it is possible to condense seven hours of golf practice into seven minutes.

The United States Army hospital conducted an experiment applying this accelerated mental process with 75 arm-and-hand amputee patients. Under hypnosis, they were given training for subordinate-handwriting (left hand for a right-handed person and vice versa). By using mental pictures, they saw themselves writing with the hand they normally did not use. Their capacity for instruction was more than doubled by using this method.

A recent winner of a divisional amateur championship,

while not using the terms of time distortion or hypnosis, described the technique exactly for reporters who questioned him about his play. He told them he had spent the week previous to the tournament putting from every angle on each of the greens. He even made written notations of the texture of the grass and of the various "breaks." He said:

"I was confident I could keep the ball in play by hitting the middle of the fairways. All that had me worried was those tricky greens. I putted them from every angle, so no matter where the committee placed the pin, I would be familiar with how the putt should be stroked.

"At night, I reviewed the notes I made. I went to sleep putting those greens. When I played in the tournament, every stroke I needed for a putt was right there in my head."

You, too, can use self-hypnosis with time distortion to practice your golf game. Before you hypnotize yourself, carefully study the sequence or motion pictures of the champions. Memorize the movements of their hands, arms, shoulders, hips, legs, and feet.

Examine them until you can close your eyes and see the swing being made. If you have any question about the mechanical movements, check your instruction books to be certain you have the point correct. The conscious mind must have no doubts when it instructs the subconscious mind during hypnosis. So, be sure to give the mental picture to your subconscious in a positive manner.

Practice with only one club during each mental session. Cary Middlecoff claims most professionals practice this way. They firmly implant the mental picture a club at a time so that it may be recalled by the subconscious feel.

When you are under self-hypnosis, transfer the identity of the professional to yourself. See yourself swing the club just as you studied the professional swing it.

Make the swing in slow motion. See every movement. Watch to make sure your left hand doesn't pronate, or your wrists roll over. See your right elbow tucked in close during the backswing.

At the top of the backswing, feel the pause. The first movement is made by your left hip and the lower part of your body. See your left heel come down firmly and your right knee slide in so there is a path for your hands to come in to make the champions' six-inch drive. Watch the follow-through as the clubhead comes on the line of flight and then comes up high.

After visualizing this in slow motion, speed it up. See yourself hitting the shot. This will produce the subconscious feel so real you will consciously feel a club in your hands. Repeat the swing time and again until you have the feeling you could not swing the club in any other way.

When you use this method of time distortion during hypnosis, you should tell yourself that there is no hurry. You have all the time you need to practice the stroke as many times as you like. This is true, for the number of practice strokes that can be made in a matter of minutes under hypnosis would require hours at a driving range.

Following a practice session with your club, review the last game you played. When you are in a state of self-hypnosis, tell yourself that in the next seven minutes you are going to replay your last game of golf. Visualize yourself stepping up to tee off and mentally follow yourself around the course, stroke by stroke, until your ball rolls into the 18th hole. Analyze and replay those shots that you made which were not satisfactory. If there was an error in distance or a flaw in your stroke, try to reason why. Try to determine what it was that caused you to allow your conscious mind from focusing its attention upon the golf ball.

You will find that after visualizing your golf game under hypnosis the scenes will become more life-like. With each practice session, there will come an increase in detail and in color. Your thought processes will seem similar to those you have when you're awake. However, they will be much more helpful because you will have an increased ability to consider your game as a whole.

When you are hypnotized, activity that seems to proceed at a normal or natural rate will actually take place with great rapidity. Even though your game appears to proceed at the customary rate, time is so compressed under hypnosis that what appears to you to be four hours of continuous play will actually take only seven "real" minutes. The reason you review your play under hypnosis is to make certain that the corrections you wish to make are implanted directly upon your subconscious mind.

The night before playing a match, if you are familiar with the course, play it mentally under hypnosis. Picture yourself on the first tee. Reason the best angle for the tee shot. See yourself swing the driver. Follow the flight of the ball to where you wish it to land. Then, select an iron to reach the green. Continue this procedure until all eighteen holes have been played.

SEVEN HOURS PRACTICE IN SEVEN MINUTES

Try to get to the practice area the day following a practice session with self-hypnosis. If this is impossible, swing your club at home without striking the ball. Swing it until you have the subconscious feel you received during hypnosis.

Close your eyes sometimes while swinging your club. This will help to promote the subconscious feel. But unless you are consciously checking some mechanical point you suspect might be wrong, you should focus your conscious attention on the ball, even with your eyes closed. This will exclude distractions from your conscious mind and let your subconscious take over.

Some of you will have trouble, however, in keeping stray thoughts out of your mind while trying to concentrate on the ball. If you do run into this trouble, switch your concentration from the ball to a visual picture of the six-inch drive. After some practice you will no longer find this necessary and your attention can be held by merely looking at the ball.

Remember, even though you remain motionless throughout hypnosis, you really participate in your mental game of golf. By utilizing time distortion you will feel you have acquired the practice effects of a similar amount of actual play in the waking state.

This mental play, when carried over into your physical play, will give you a feeling of confidence. Every time you step up to a tee you will feel that this particular shot has already been made in advance. This feeling of confidence will be reflected in a lower golf score and a more relaxed and enjoyable game.

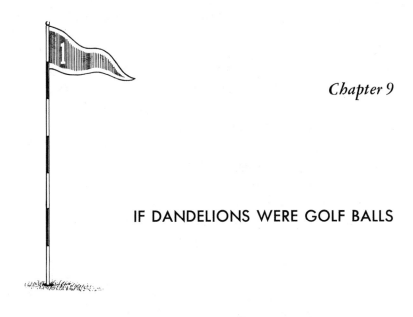

IF DANDELIONS WERE GOLF BALLS

"The National Open is not won, it is lost."

"The way to win a tournament is to come in early with a respectable score and let the rest of the field defeat itself trying to beat you."

"A golfer's toughest opponent is himself."

"Don't beat yourself, make the other fellow do it."

All of these quotations refer to tension. Tension is the end product of fear, or, as Jules Platte and Herb Graffis declared in their book, *Golf Practice,* "The sad truth is that much of the potential value of practice is destroyed by tension ... bane of many a golfer. Most tension is caused by fear.

"The average golfer doesn't know how to make a difficult shot, so he's afraid to make it. Under pressure of competition, the expert, on the other hand, fears a shot he knows won't come off exactly right, so he tenses and locks.

"Both the ordinary golfer and star know fear."

Have you ever been chided by a golf instructor who has told you not to fear hitting the golf ball because it can't hit back? Then, what is there about that small, dimpled, white ball that can make you freeze on a shot?

Actually, it's not the ball you're afraid of, but what's going to happen when you hit it. You know there is at least a 50-50 chance that when your clubhead comes into contact with the ball, it won't do what you wanted it to do. If it doesn't, a penalty is involved. When a penalty is involved, your muscles tense and you're off on your stroke. When you're off on your stroke, a penalty is involved. When a penalty is involved—and so on, ad infinitum.

An amusing story concerns a golfer who was so seriously certain he could swing perfectly at a dandelion that he placed one on top of his ball every time he stepped up to the tee. Unfortunately, he always seemed to remember that underneath it was a ball, not a stem. Then he would remark ruefully, "If I could only fool myself into believing it was really a dandelion, I would have this game licked."

Have you ever taken a practice swing at a dandelion? Do you remember being about 150 yards from a green, waiting for the foursome ahead to hole out? Seeing a dandelion growing in the grass, you pretended it was a golf ball. You addressed it properly, brought your club down, and sent the yellow head flying toward the green. The swing was "sweet" and the finish of your stroke was high and stylish. If the dandelion had been a golf ball, it would have nestled right up close to the pin.

How often have you heard the remark, "When I take a practice swing, I feel everything is just right. But the moment I stand up to the ball, I freeze." Or perhaps you've heard the reverse comment, "He played like he was unconscious."

A good example of unconscious playing happened in 1955 when Jack Fleck, called the "Cinderella-man" of golf, won the U. S. National Open in San Francisco.

Fleck started his golf career as a caddy in Davenport, Iowa. He advanced from shopboy to assistant pro to head professional.

Following a three-year stretch in the Navy, Fleck hit the pro trail. He returned home to operate a driving range and took time out from his busy schedule to qualify for the National Open. He lasted through the cuts, but the only mention he received in the newspapers was that of an "also entered."

Gene Sarazen was at the microphone covering the final day of play. Ben Hogan posted a 72-hole total of 277. A quick check of the big names showed there was none within striking distance. Sarazen announced Hogan as the winner.

The forgotten man, Jack Fleck, was still on the course at the time. He was at the 14th, and needed two pars and two birdies on the remaining tough holes for a tie.

By the time he had reached the 18th tee, he had picked up two pars and one birdie. He needed only one more birdie for a tie.

He stepped up to the tee, swung his club, hit the ball, and drove into the rough — not the neatly manicured rough of the country club set, but the deep, rugged rough used to test the skill of the champions. The gallery, intent upon their local idol, Hogan, didn't even know he was still in contention. He had been counted out by everyone but himself.

Alone with his caddy in the deep rough, Fleck asked for a four iron. He hit the ball and it arched for the green. It took the bite and pulled up seven feet from the pin. There weren't many spectators there to watch Fleck tap it in for his birdie.

After the play-off, Ike Granger handed Fleck the U. S. Open trophy. It was the first one he had ever received in all the time he had been playing golf.

How did he do it? Here is the way Fleck described it to the eager sports writers who were waiting to write the story of the rags-to-riches golf pro.

"It happened on the fifth, after I had made four pars. I can't exactly describe it, but as I looked at the putt, the hole looked as big as a washtub. I suddenly became convinced I couldn't miss. Actually, I tried four or five practice swings to see if the sensation remained. It did, and from then on, throughout the tournament and play-off, I hit the ball and putted like I had never hit or putted before.

"All I tried to do was keep the sensation by not questioning it. I played one shot after the other, one hole after another, trying not to think of what was ahead. I felt as long as the sensation stayed with me, I couldn't do anything wrong."

What was this sensation Fleck claimed he felt? It was the subconscious feel. It was the complete subconscious control of his muscles used in the golf stroke.

Fleck, by not trying to question the sensation, managed to keep his conscious mind from interfering with the subconscious feel. He could just as accurately have described the sensation as self-hypnosis which is the fixation of the conscious mind on a single objective.

Fleck's remarkable game was a good example of letting your subconscious override any doubts or fears. But, as you know, tension can affect even the best of the pros.

If you can recall the 1959-60 *Championship Golf* television series, you will remember that Cary Middlecoff and Mike Souchak defeated a full field of champions and entered a 36-hole play-off. They seesawed through 35 holes, and Dr. Middlecoff was one-up when they came to the last green. He holed out for a par four.

Souchak had a three-foot birdie putt to make. If he dropped it, he would tie the match and continue for a possible win.

The three-footer was worth $15,000. Five thousand dollars a foot was the difference between the first place $37,500 and second-place money.

There wasn't a sound from the gallery, even though Souchak took a lot of time getting the line. It appeared to be almost a straight putt. Finally, he addressed the ball, and tapped it. It rolled one foot, then another, and was going straight toward the hole. It finally got there—and pulled to the left. The game was over.

Most average golfers figure they could make putts for $5,000 a foot, at least up to three feet. But how many three-footers have you missed in friendly matches when you only had a dime riding on them?

Just as an experiment, try the following: Drop six balls on the practice green, then push a tee on the grass six feet away. Now, see how close you can lag the balls to the tee.

Next, drop six balls on the practice green six feet from the hole. See how many of these you can drop in. How many were closer when lagging for the tee than going for the hole?

For the acid test, make a wager with a friend after he has tried the same experiment as to how many he can "ace." He'll probably wonder what happened to that smooth stroke he had when he was only lagging them to the tee.

Chick Evans, the bright golfing star of the 20's, wrote: "Putts are short because of hesitation. Hesitation is fear."

Now, do you understand what happens when the conscious mind is allowed to enter the stroke? When it is aware that a penalty is involved, it creates fear which turns into muscle tension.

"But," you ask, "why do I get so shook up about a shot that doesn't seem to bother my opponent at all?"

The answer may possibly be found in a story told about a minister playing with a member of his congregation.

IF DANDELIONS WERE GOLF BALLS

The member was having a bad day, and finally lost his temper and began swearing.

Seeking to make a point of self-control, the minister said, "John, I notice that most good players do not resort to swearing."

The frustrated player exploded: "What in the bankety-blank have they got to swear about?"

So you see, an insignificant problem for one person may seem insurmountable by another. Each person carries his own yardstick to measure his personal fears and anxieties.

The poor player, aware of his inadequacies, is more keenly aware of the penalties. The out-of-bounds markers appear closer and the traps deeper. The more he dwells upon what can go wrong, the more tension mounts in his conscious mind. This creates a vicious circle that goes on and on.

The only antidote for the poison of fear is confidence. In order to become confident, you must have a swing on which you can rely. This happens only when your swing is controlled by your subconscious mind.

Chapter 10

MENTAL BUNKERS

"What did I do wrong?"

"You peeked. Next time keep your head down."

This advice, as the cure-all for any golf ailment, probably originated with the first shepherds who whacked their feather-filled leather bags along the Scottish links. And ever since then it has been a controversial subject— even among the experts. What causes the head to move and how long must it remain fixed are two questions that cause most of the controversy.

Jackie Burke states: "The old saw about keeping your eye on the ball is worthless. Before you hit the ball, I defy you to take your eyes off it. After you've hit it, what difference does it make where you look?"

The point that Burke is trying to make is that your eyes can be fastened upon the ball, and still your head can move up, down, or sideways. It is also possible to keep your eyes closed or (as trickshot artists do) completely turn your head away and still hit the ball.

All that is necessary is to keep your head as the axis for the swing. It must remain fixed so that the mechanical movements can be made repeatedly and automatically.

Johnny Revolta explains it this way: "The average beginner has a tendency to raise and move the head because he consciously or unconsciously feels he must scoop the ball to get it in the air. As a result, his weight goes to the right, pulling his head up."

This is a mechanical error. It can be corrected by the right visual image of the swing. There is no scooping movement in the champions' six-inch drive.

Tommy Armour says, "All the fancy theories and complexities of the golf swing that I've heard about are not nearly as important as the simple essential of keeping your head steady." He goes on to suggest that the average player moves his head because of an anxiety to see where the ball is going. This anxiety is particularly noticeable in putting, which causes the shoulders to be pulled off line, thus causing the putt to roll to the left of the cup.

The advice to keep the head down can be overemphasized, just as any other golf instruction. If the head is held rigid, it restricts body movement.

Paul Runyan, Southern California teaching pro, says, "Keeping your eyes on the ball may help you maintain your head on the same level, but it is no guarantee your head will be in the proper position. I have seen golfers stare intently at the ball, and yet come up—or down— with the stroke. Keeping the head level, whether it be up or down, makes better sense."

However, whether the advice is to "keep your eyes on the ball," "keep your head down," or "keep your head level," it is about as effective as telling you that the trouble is the "wheels aren't moving" when you are in a stalled automobile. They are statements of effect rather than cause, and most of the self-abusive language heard on the course comes from golfers berating themselves for this fault.

You do not deliberately lift your head to spoil the shot. Why is it, then, that the error so consistently creeps into your play?

It is because a mental block has been set up in your subconscious mind. It prevents you from doing what you consciously want to do. It is created through fear and tension, which, in turn, produce muscle contractions.

To eliminate the effect (head movement), the cause (fear and tension) must first be removed.

Confidence banishes fear. Golf confidence is created by the subconscious feel. It allows the conscious mind to concentrate upon the ball and your subconscious to produce the automatic swing.

By this time you're probably thinking the subconscious feel is a golf cure-all. Well, that's exactly what it is. It is the only way you can discover the automatic swing used by the champions.

Once you've learned it through hypnosis and committed

it to your subconscious mind through practice, you *must* play better golf.

Of course, there's always the chance you might lose this feel during play. Should you lose it once you have discovered it, you can quickly reactivate it through practice swings. No penalty is involved, and the conscious mind will not interfere.

It is practice, both mental and physical, and using one club at a time that builds confidence for you. As soon as you activate the subconscious feel during practice, you can be sure that when you address the ball you will hit it right. This relieves the fear in your conscious mind concerning a penalty. You will be able to focus your attention upon the ball and play the stroke subconsciously.

One common way you can destroy the subconscious feel is to miss a shot, and then ask yourself, "What did I do wrong?"

You are committing a serious psychological error when you put doubt into your play. This negative thinking creates fear and results in a bad game.

Once Walter Hagen missed a short putt, and someone close to him started to sympathize. Hagen would have none of it, and said: "We all miss those short putts, and I am not going to worry about this one. Bye and bye, I will make it up with a long one. If I stopped to think about such minor details, I might get it into my head that my putting touch is at fault, and this is exactly what I don't want to do."

If a putt or shot should not come off as expected, dismiss it from your mind. Don't take your game apart on the course. Do your thinking in the practice area.

When you approach the next shot, take a practice swing to activate the subconscious feel. If you still feel doubtful, take several practice swings until your confidence returns.

Do not become discouraged. Even professionals, with their knowledge of the game and constant practice, still have bad days. What causes them and how you can avoid them is very important to your game.

An obvious (but often overlooked) truth is that a bad day of golf starts with only one bad shot. At the most, it should only cost a single stroke. If it costs more, it is because you have allowed the effect of it to negatively condition your thinking. You use it as an omen for your entire game.

If you can hit good shots in the practice area or play a number of good strokes during a round, you have only your unchecked mental processes to blame if you allow one bad shot to spoil your entire day.

Tommy Bolt, dubbed "Terrible Tempered Tommy" by the press, and who is known as "King of the Club Throwers," says he figures he is going to make a certain number of bad shots during any round and allows for them. He claims his habit of throwing clubs is to let off steam. This explosion lets him forget the bad shot and approach the next one with determination to do better.

While club throwing is frowned upon, and Bolt has paid considerably in fines for his temper during tournament play, psychologists approve of letting off steam.

In a recent Antarctic expedition, Captain C. S. Mullin, Navy neuropsychiatrist, noted that the men who engaged in horseplay, swearing and raucous insults were less affected by tension than the men who did not.

Don't allow a single bad shot to start a chain reaction. Many players, overly concerned that a misplayed shot has cost them a hole or put them a stroke behind their opponent, try to make it up on the next shot.

The unwritten rule of golf is that a misplayed shot costs a stroke. It is part of the game, like getting a deuce in the hole in stud poker. Trying to bluff your way out is a good way to go broke.

Remember to play the course, not your opponent. The deciding factor in winning a game is not how many balls you hit well, but how many you hit badly. You will win more matches by your opponent's errors than by your own success.

One bad shot followed by another makes a duffer. One bad shot does not make you a poor golfer. The champions often play one or more poorly hit shots in a round. When an error sneaks into their play, their only concern is that they do not repeat it.

If you want to be a champion, then swing like a champion, play like a champion, think like a champion. Realize that a bad shot is caused by a mental lapse and dismiss it from your mind. Accept the penalty and approach the hole with confidence.

Force the memory of the bad shot from your conscious mind by focusing your attention upon the ball as you play the next shot. Activate the subconscious feel by practice swings before you hit it. In this way you will gain the needed confidence.

MENTAL BUNKERS

One way to turn a bad shot into a bad day is to doubt your ability. Say to yourself, "I haven't got it today." You can assure failure by suspecting something is wrong with your grip, stance or swing. Then you will fail to trust the subconscious feel and blow the next shot by using conscious effort to "force" a better score. Forget about how many good shots you have made and concentrate on the bad ones. Cap it off by complaining about your lousy luck. If you don't give golf up after this, there's a good chance the rest of your foursome will give you up.

To help erase the memory of an out-of-bounds drive, think of it as a three-foot putt. For some reason, there isn't the despair in missing a three-footer as there is in losing a 200-yard drive. Of course there is a certain amount of anger.

The next time you send one into a wooded rough, pick out the easiest way back to the fairway. Select a spot where a good approach can be made to the green. Tell yourself, "If I can hit that spot, I can lay the next one dead to the pin. With one putt, this error will not cost me anything." Dismiss everything from your mind except getting back to the fairway. This mental play is the technique used by the champions.

One of the most dismaying shots you can make is one that is topped or stubbed near the green. It is infuriating because you know it was caused by carelessness. You are so anxious to get this shot behind you that you often hurry the second shot, thus creating the chance that the same carelessness will occur.

When you miss a pitch or chip shot, take plenty of time

before playing the next one. The same holds true for a missed putt. Should you feel particularly anxious, walk completely away from the ball until you regain your composure. When you return, your conscious mind will not interfere with the subconscious control of your stroke.

If you have a high handicap, you can improve your game by mentally re-evaluating the course as you play. Change the pars to bogey pars.

For example, if you score around 100, and the course is rated at 72, there is a 28-stroke difference between your score and par. If you want to make 90, this will leave you 18 strokes for a bogey par on every hole.

A 4-par hole is from 251 to 445 yards, with the average being under 400 yards. Try to get a 175-yard drive on your first stroke. Next, use your 4-iron or 3-wood to go another 150 yards. Then, try for a 75-yard pitch. This will put you on the green. With two putts, you're down for a bogey par. If you pay careful attention to chips and pitches, you may get within one putt on some holes. Then, you can put one stroke in your back pocket to be used in the event you get into trouble later on in the game.

If you play the course one hole at a time, either borrowing or saving "back-pocket strokes," you can score 90 easily.

If you want to try for 80, this will leave you eight spares. They should be spent on the tough, long holes. If you keep a record of where you had to use them, you will know on which clubs you need more practice.

Remember, even the tournament pros don't shoot all of their rounds on sub-par figures.

MENTAL BUNKERS

The Vardon Trophy for the best performance average for men was won by Art Wall with 70.35, Bob Rosburg with 70.11, Dow Finsterwald with 70.29, Cary Middlecoff with 70.35, Sam Snead with 69.86, E. J. "Dutch" Harrison with 70.41, and Lloyd Mangrum with 70.22.

These figures are for the world's greatest players during their best years. So, when you are shooting in the high 70's or low 80's, you are keeping pretty good company.

After you have been playing well, you will still have days when things go all to pieces. It may start right on the first tee, or at any time during the round. No matter how diligently you try to re-activate the subconscious feel, it is gone.

When this happens, there is a good chance you have been negatively hypnotized right on the course. This is called involuntary hypnosis and is a common occurrence. The requisites needed to produce hypnosis are quiet surroundings, a relaxed body and the conscious mind concentrating upon a single thought or object.

Now, put yourself on the players' bench at a tee. You're stretched out, relaxed and waiting your turn to drive.

One of the players takes his stance. The rest of you remain courteously quiet. Your attention is focused upon him as he takes his practice swing and then hits the ball.

The requirements for producing hypnosis are all there. How it can affect your game is described by Dick Mayer, in his book, *How To Think and Swing Like a Golf Champion.* He writes: "If you make any mistakes, make sure they are your own, not an error you have picked up from another player.

"When another player is on the tee, I find something

else to do, rather than watch him. I pick out somebody in the gallery to look at, or some object, or think about my own drive.

"Unless the player happens to be someone like Sam Snead, whose rhythm and timing I would like to have sneak into my swing, I simply divorce myself from the sight and sound of anyone else's tee shot.

"For if I paid attention to his swing, I may pick up his errors."

There is an additional danger in watching another player. If he gets a long drive, you may consciously try to extend yourself to match it, rather than focusing your conscious mind in order to produce the automatic swing. Or, should he not get a good shot, you may implant the suggestion of his poor play in your own subconscious.

Jackie Burke warns: "Never underestimate the power of suggestion in a round of golf. How often have you seen a golfer being painfully careful not to hit a ball out of bounds, wind up doing just that?

"Few people shank a ball who did not have a shank in mind before they hit. Few people are chronic slicers who do not have a fear of a slice, who do not have an apparition of it parade across their imagination before each and every shot they hit."

Side bets for "long ball" and "closest to" often throw you off your game. You must be careful not to let the fear of a penalty (the bet) enter your conscious thoughts during the swing. If it does, you will stretch or steer the ball consciously and be headed for trouble.

Remember, when your conscious mind gets into the act, it activates unwanted muscles that wreck your golf swing.

MENTAL BUNKERS

The only time to accept a long ball bet is when you have the honor at the tee. Concentrate particularly on excluding distractions from your conscious mind by focusing its attention upon the ball so as to allow your subconscious mind to play the stroke automatically. If you get a straight hit, it will invariably cause your opponent to stretch himself into trouble.

Johnny Revolta counsels: "There's an advantage in shooting first. If you get a good shot, the average player will extend himself to duplicate it. On the other hand, if your opponent outdrives you, take advantage of it. You will have the first shot on the fairway. Make it good. He may match you the first time, but, sooner or later, he'll crack under the pressure."

At one time or the other you have used "gamesmanship" on the course. This is psychology used to defeat your opponent by causing him to tense up. You do it by carefully pointing out a particularly bad stretch of rough, out-of-bounds markers, or water hazards, or by saying, "Watch these greens. They're fast and tricky." This will inevitably cause your opponent to freeze.

You have to remember, however, when using gamesmanship tactics, to be careful not to sow the seed of doubt in your own mind. Otherwise, your own game will be effected, and what kind of psychology is that?

The only answer to consistent golf is to play within yourself. By employing self-hypnosis to produce the subconscious feel, you will know exactly what each of your clubs will do. This makes your swing automatic and your game more enjoyable.

Golf is that simple.

Consistently good golf is played with the automatic
swing. The only way your stroke can become automatic
is by controlling your subconscious mind through the use
of hypnosis.

Your conscious mind uses mental pictures to graphically
impress your subconscious with the correct mechanical
movements of the golf swing. This is turned into subconscious feel which is the champions' secret of both
physical and mental play.

No therapy, theory or technique is of value unless you
surrender yourself to it. No one can do your thinking for
you. You are the only one who can give yourself the
subconscious feel, and you can find it in only one way —

by practicing self-hypnosis.

A bridge, a building, a painting, and a song are all created in the mind, but they do not become realities until their creators translate their thoughts into action. You can't become a good golfer by just thinking or wishing. You must spend time in the practice area. Champions master their stroke and the game through hard work. Now that you know what you are seeking and have the instructions on how to achieve it, your job is made easier for you.

The mental side of golf is the blue print; practice is the construction. The time required for both mental and physical play can be greatly reduced by using time distortion during hypnosis. However, the subconscious feel can only be found through practice. Your golf stroke, like your mind, improves with use. If you will give only a small portion of your future time to discovering the subconscious feel, the reward of better golf will be yours.

Talk about your new goals and aspirations with your friends. By repeating them, you will implant these ideas more deeply in your mind. You will find they become clearer and more defined as you explain them. Speak of your goal with confidence. Know what you are going to do, how you are going to do it, and then do it.

There will always be those who scoff at any new idea as being a gimmick. These scoffers are usually unwilling to spend the time and effort to examine and try a new idea. The fact that you have read this book is evidence that you have an open mind. Sufficient proof has been offered to show that better golf can be achieved through self-hypnosis. If you accept this proof, then you are on your way to better golf.

The challenge of golf is to the individual. You wouldn't have it any other way. A match is played with an opponent, but you also constantly play against yourself. Golf could be played with mechanical contrivances to drive the ball accurately and spring-loaded putters to sink the ball on every shot. But the enjoyment of golf would be lost if you received the golf stroke and the ability to make it as a gift. All you ask of the game is the knowledge of how you can master it for yourself. You don't want odds to win; you want to win with your own ability. If this were not true, you would be satisfied with your handicap.

There is no way the subconscious feel can be described exactly. Can anyone accurately describe the taste of cherry pop to you? It can only be described by comparing it to something else. The only way to experience the subconscious feel is to induce it yourself. Once you induce it, it will be as enlightening as a light turned on in a dark room. You will recognize it because you have been seeking it since the first day you swung a golf club. You will know it from the satisfaction of the result. And should you lose it on a stroke, you will recognize it as you would a sudden discord in music or a misstep in dancing.

The use of self-hypnosis to master the golf stroke is not difficult, but it is not a gift. You must earn it through practice. Constant repetition will make it more difficult for your conscious mind to interfere and cause you to lose the subconscious feel when playing.

Your goal is to make the golf stroke as natural as

walking or driving a car. It's up to you to bring subconscious control to your game.

Perhaps the following question-and-answer section will help you solve some problem that is bothering you about self-hypnosis or golf:

Q: Are you certain there isn't something more to inducing self-hypnosis than the simple instructions you have given?

A: Absolutely certain. You may check other books if you like, but you will find the means of producing hypnosis are exactly the same.

Q: I talked about using self-hypnosis to improve my golf with some friends. They said it's impossible. Is it?

A: The use of hypnosis in golf represents a new application of this science. If your friends have not read this book, they cannot give you a valid opinion. If this book has made sense to you, why don't you try it and be your own judge?

Q: What is the difference between self-hypnosis and positive thinking? It seems to me they are the same thing.

A: The two terms are often confused as being the same. Positive thinking deals only with the conscious mind. This is just the first step in self-hypnosis. The second step is to transfer these positive thoughts from the conscious to the subconscious through the use of hypnosis. When applied to golf, it produces the subconscious feel.

Q: If professional golf players use self-hypnosis, why don't they say anything about it? Maybe you're twisting their words around to make it look like they do.

A: Many professionals do refer to hypnosis. Bobby Jones described his iron-play as "so exceptional I felt I must have been hypnotized." Don't blame the pros if they don't recognize hypnosis. It has only been within the past few years that it has been recognized by medical societies.

Q: I was so anxious to learn golf, I took lessons from a pro. Until I learned about self-hypnosis, I didn't know what he was talking about when he tried to describe the mental side of golf. I always thought it was just a physical act. Now we spend more time talking than we do hitting, and I'm coming along just fine. Is there any specific thing I should do in order to improve my game?

A: Go even further. Use time distortion and mental imagery when you practice. See if you don't come along even faster.

Q: Manipulation of time during hypnosis intrigues me. Where can I find more information about it?

A: One of the best books on the subject is *Time Distortion In Hypnosis* by Linn F. Cooper, M.D. and Milton H. Erickson, M.D.

Q: I tried self-hypnosis, but it isn't curing my hurried backswing. I realize that this is a physical movement and doesn't concern the mental part of the game. Have you any suggestions to remedy this?

A: Yes. You know that all muscle movements, voluntary and involuntary, are controlled by your mind. Your hurried backswing is the result of conscious effort. Once you have discovered the subconscious feel, your backswing won't be hurried. The best way to get this subconscious feel is to consciously study the movements of the experts. A movie would be a great help to you in showing how they pause at the top of their swing. When you visualize and copy this, your trouble will be over.

Q: You said that tensions produce unwanted muscular action. Do you have any actual proof of this?

A: Northrop Aviation researchers conducted scientific tests to determine the amount of muscle strain produced by tension in order to learn its effect upon astronauts for space travel.

Tiny electrodes were taped to the bodies of test pilots. The results were recorded upon a telemeter. When the pilots were placed in a simulated space ship and told they were to control it, the computer showed only a quarter of a degree drop in temperatures and moderate muscle tension.

Then they were told something had gone wrong, and they were in possible danger. Muscle tension increased four times and some temperatures dropped two degrees. The men were unable to react or perform with normal efficiency.

Q: I have been able to induce self-hypnosis, and it has worked wonders for my game. However, there are days when I am so keyed up, I just can't get it to work. When this happens, I go back to the way I used to play, which wasn't good. What can I do about it?

A: Even pros have days when personal or business problems are more pressing than golf. When your conscious mind is filled with these problems, you will have difficulty concentrating upon your game. If you use self-hypnosis to help solve some of these other problems, it will give you more time for your golf thoughts.

Q: I have a friend who says nobody can hypnotize him. Do you think he could be hypnotized?

A: I can't think of anyone who would want to hypnotize him against his wishes. Under the right conditions he can be hypnotized if he is motivated to be hypnotized. The only requirement is a willingness on his part.

Q: I have seen some of the big time pros pull boners. What happened to their mental game?

A: Men are human, not machines. Golf is a game, not a test of physical fitness or endurance. Mike Souchak said: "I don't believe I have ever played a round of golf without making a mental error, and what's more, I don't think anyone has. Usually, it's a loss of concentration."

Pros make only one mistake at a time if they stay up in the money. It's the dub who lets one mistake disturb him so that he makes another. One bad shot won't hurt you if you don't follow it with a second or third.

Q: How can I tell if I am using my conscious or subconscious mind when I play golf?

A: Usually the score card will tell you if you are letting your conscious mind control the stroke. If you feel any strain or muscle tension, you can be sure your conscious mind has gotten into the act. The subconsious feel is almost effortless.

Q: I have heard it said that if you are hypnotized too many times, it will make your mind weak. Is this true?

A: In hypnosis you concentrate thoughts along constructive channels. Knowing how to concentrate will improve your mind and general mental attitude rather than weaken it.

Q: I am still puzzled about the subconscious feel. Can you describe it a little more fully for me?

A: If, when you dance, you let your feet react subconsciously to the rhythm of the music, you are experiencing the subconscious feel. If you try to consciously make certain steps as you do when you are learning to dance, the motions will be jerky. It is the subconscious feel that makes a good dancer. It is the same subconscious feel that will make you a good golfer.

Q: I am interested in learning more about self-hypnosis. Can you recommend a good book?

A. You might like to read *A Practical Guide to Self-Hypnosis* by Melvin Powers. In this book Mr. Powers not only thoroughly explains self-hypnosis but gives a thoughtful investigation into the motivation for its application.

Q: Has hypnosis been applied to sports other than golf?

A: Yes. It has been used in sports as varied as bowling, tennis, baseball, football, skiing, archery, swimming, basketball and track.

Dr. Huber Grimm, team physician of the Seattle University basketball team, recently related the results when Dave Mills, a six-foot five-inch, junior forward, asked for his help because he "froze" during competition. He had been benched on the eve of the West Coast Athletic Conference tournament in San Francisco. Spectators made Mills so fearful that he was afraid he would make mistakes — and in this frame of mind, of course, he did. Under hypnosis, Dr. Grimm suggested to Dave that he would be unaware of the spectators, completely relaxed and would play exceedingly well. Dr. Grimm asked coach Vince Cazzeta to allow Dave to play and the result was astounding. Mills scored 60 points and cleared 63 rebounds in a single game, and his brilliant play led to his selection on the all-tournament team.

"All I did was free his spirit," Dr. Grimm reported. "He was in need of confidence, and I gave it to him through hypnosis." The Associated Press told the story as follows: "Dave Mills, a vacuum cleaner off the backboards, led a fast-breaking Seattle University team to victory last night. It was hard to recognize Mills as the same player who has been with the Chieftans all year."

Dr. William S. Kroger, a pioneer in hypnosis, undertook to improve the batting of a professional baseball player with equally sensational results. The player had been "beaned," and his fear of a recurrence was so strong that he became "plate shy." He had changed his batting stance so that he always had "one foot in the bucket" so that he could back away from the plate more quickly. He was given a posthypnotic suggestion that such an event happening again was exceedingly remote, and this was amplified by suggestions of confidence that he would immediately start slugging as well as ever. His batting average soared immediately.

Dr. Michio Ikai, professor of physiology at Tokyo University, and Dr. Arthur H. Steinhaus of the George Williams College Laboratory of Physiology Research in Physical Education, Chicago, have proved that trackmen can far surpass their best previous times under hypnosis.

Their tests, incidentally, proved that there is no danger of an athlete going beyond his physiologic limit while bettering his former marks. They attribute the superior performances to the removal of inhibitions which psychologically prevent an athlete from doing his best. This report was made before the International Congress on Health and Fitness in the Modern World held in Rome during the last Olympic games.

All reports, as a matter of fact, show that athletic performances are improved by psychological, not physical, means, and that built-in automatic reflexes protect the athlete against the danger of overexertion at all levels of awareness — hypnotic or nonhypnotic.

In conclusion, there is all the evidence needed that you can help your golf game, as well as any other in which you wish to excel, through the use of hypnosis.

Q: I have heard there is a record that hypnotizes you and gives you posthypnotic suggestions to improve your golf game. Can this be effective?

A. Yes. Melvin Powers, one of the leading professional hypnotists in Los Angeles who advocates the use of self-hypsosis, has made such a hypnotic golf record. It is called *Golf Like a Pro* and it can be extremely effective in improving your golf game and adding to your confidence. This 33⅓ RPM record, which sells for $7, can be obtained through your golf shop or directly from the Wilshire Book Company, 12015 Sherman Road, No. Hollywood, California 91605.

MELVIN POWERS SELF-IMPROVEMENT LIBRARY

ASTROLOGY

_____ ASTROLOGY: HOW TO CHART YOUR HOROSCOPE *Max Heindel*	5.00
_____ ASTROLOGY AND SEXUAL ANALYSIS *Morris C. Goodman*	5.00
_____ ASTROLOGY MADE EASY *Astarte*	3.00
_____ ASTROLOGY MADE PRACTICAL *Alexandra Kayhle*	3.00
_____ ASTROLOGY, ROMANCE, YOU AND THE STARS *Anthony Norvell*	4.00
_____ MY WORLD OF ASTROLOGY *Sydney Omarr*	7.00
_____ THOUGHT DIAL *Sydney Omarr*	4.00
_____ WHAT THE STARS REVEAL ABOUT THE MEN IN YOUR LIFE *Thelma White*	3.00

BRIDGE

_____ BRIDGE BIDDING MADE EASY *Edwin B. Kantar*	10.00
_____ BRIDGE CONVENTIONS *Edwin B. Kantar*	7.00
_____ BRIDGE HUMOR *Edwin B. Kantar*	5.00
_____ COMPETITIVE BIDDING IN MODERN BRIDGE *Edgar Kaplan*	7.00
_____ DEFENSIVE BRIDGE PLAY COMPLETE *Edwin B. Kantar*	15.00
_____ GAMESMAN BRIDGE—Play Better with Kantar *Edwin B. Kantar*	5.00
_____ HOW TO IMPROVE YOUR BRIDGE *Alfred Sheinwold*	5.00
_____ IMPROVING YOUR BIDDING SKILLS *Edwin B. Kantar*	4.00
_____ INTRODUCTION TO DECLARER'S PLAY *Edwin B. Kantar*	5.00
_____ INTRODUCTION TO DEFENDER'S PLAY *Edwin B. Kantar*	3.00
_____ KANTAR FOR THE DEFENSE *Edwin B. Kantar*	7.00
_____ KANTAR FOR THE DEFENSE VOLUME 2 *Edwin B. Kantar*	7.00
_____ SHORT CUT TO WINNING BRIDGE *Alfred Sheinwold*	3.00
_____ TEST YOUR BRIDGE PLAY *Edwin B. Kantar*	5.00
_____ VOLUME 2—TEST YOUR BRIDGE PLAY *Edwin B. Kantar*	5.00
_____ WINNING DECLARER PLAY *Dorothy Hayden Truscott*	5.00

BUSINESS, STUDY & REFERENCE

_____ CONVERSATION MADE EASY *Elliot Russell*	4.00
_____ EXAM SECRET *Dennis B. Jackson*	3.00
_____ FIX-IT BOOK *Arthur Symons*	2.00
_____ HOW TO DEVELOP A BETTER SPEAKING VOICE *M. Hellier*	4.00
_____ HOW TO SELF-PUBLISH YOUR BOOK & MAKE IT A BEST SELLER *Melvin Powers*	10.00
_____ INCREASE YOUR LEARNING POWER *Geoffrey A. Dudley*	3.00
_____ PRACTICAL GUIDE TO BETTER CONCENTRATION *Melvin Powers*	3.00
_____ PRACTICAL GUIDE TO PUBLIC SPEAKING *Maurice Forley*	5.00
_____ 7 DAYS TO FASTER READING *William S. Schaill*	3.00
_____ SONGWRITERS' RHYMING DICTIONARY *Jane Shaw Whitfield*	7.00
_____ SPELLING MADE EASY *Lester D. Basch & Dr. Milton Finkelstein*	3.00
_____ STUDENT'S GUIDE TO BETTER GRADES *J. A. Rickard*	3.00
_____ TEST YOURSELF—Find Your Hidden Talent *Jack Shafer*	3.00
_____ YOUR WILL & WHAT TO DO ABOUT IT *Attorney Samuel G. Kling*	4.00

CALLIGRAPHY

_____ ADVANCED CALLIGRAPHY *Katherine Jeffares*	7.00
_____ CALLIGRAPHER'S REFERENCE BOOK *Anne Leptich & Jacque Evans*	7.00
_____ CALLIGRAPHY—The Art of Beautiful Writing *Katherine Jeffares*	7.00
_____ CALLIGRAPHY FOR FUN & PROFIT *Anne Leptich & Jacque Evans*	7.00
_____ CALLIGRAPHY MADE EASY *Tina Serafini*	7.00

CHESS & CHECKERS

_____ BEGINNER'S GUIDE TO WINNING CHESS *Fred Reinfeld*	5.00
_____ CHESS IN TEN EASY LESSONS *Larry Evans*	5.00
_____ CHESS MADE EASY *Milton L. Hanauer*	3.00
_____ CHESS PROBLEMS FOR BEGINNERS *edited by Fred Reinfeld*	2.00
_____ CHESS SECRETS REVEALED *Fred Reinfeld*	2.00
_____ CHESS TACTICS FOR BEGINNERS *edited by Fred Reinfeld*	4.00
_____ CHESS THEORY & PRACTICE *Morry & Mitchell*	2.00
_____ HOW TO WIN AT CHECKERS *Fred Reinfeld*	3.00
_____ 1001 BRILLIANT WAYS TO CHECKMATE *Fred Reinfeld*	5.00
_____ 1001 WINNING CHESS SACRIFICES & COMBINATIONS *Fred Reinfeld*	5.00

____ HOW YOU CAN BEAT THE RACES *Jack Kavanagh*	5.00
____ MAKING MONEY AT THE RACES *David Barr*	5.00
____ PAYDAY AT THE RACES *Les Conklin*	3.00
____ SMART HANDICAPPING MADE EASY *William Bauman*	5.00
____ SUCCESS AT THE HARNESS RACES *Barry Meadow*	5.00
____ WINNING AT THE HARNESS RACES—An Expert's Guide *Nick Cammarano*	5.00

HUMOR

____ HOW TO FLATTEN YOUR TUSH *Coach Marge Reardon*	2.00
____ HOW TO MAKE LOVE TO YOURSELF *Ron Stevens & Joy Grdnic*	3.00
____ JOKE TELLER'S HANDBOOK *Bob Orben*	5.00
____ JOKES FOR ALL OCCASIONS *Al Schock*	5.00
____ 2000 NEW LAUGHS FOR SPEAKERS *Bob Orben*	5.00
____ 2,500 JOKES TO START 'EM LAUGHING *Bob Orben*	5.00

HYPNOTISM

____ ADVANCED TECHNIQUES OF HYPNOSIS *Melvin Powers*	3.00
____ BRAINWASHING AND THE CULTS *Paul A. Verdier, Ph.D.*	3.00
____ CHILDBIRTH WITH HYPNOSIS *William S. Kroger, M.D.*	5.00
____ HOW TO SOLVE Your Sex Problems with Self-Hypnosis *Frank S. Caprio, M.D.*	5.00
____ HOW TO STOP SMOKING THRU SELF-HYPNOSIS *Leslie M. LeCron*	3.00
____ HOW TO USE AUTO-SUGGESTION EFFECTIVELY *John Duckworth*	3.00
____ HOW YOU CAN BOWL BETTER USING SELF-HYPNOSIS *Jack Heise*	4.00
____ HOW YOU CAN PLAY BETTER GOLF USING SELF-HYPNOSIS *Jack Heise*	3.00
____ HYPNOSIS AND SELF-HYPNOSIS *Bernard Hollander, M.D.*	5.00
____ HYPNOTISM *(Originally published in 1893) Carl Sextus*	5.00
____ HYPNOTISM & PSYCHIC PHENOMENA *Simeon Edmunds*	4.00
____ HYPNOTISM MADE EASY *Dr. Ralph Winn*	3.00
____ HYPNOTISM MADE PRACTICAL *Louis Orton*	5.00
____ HYPNOTISM REVEALED *Melvin Powers*	2.00
____ HYPNOTISM TODAY *Leslie LeCron and Jean Bordeaux, Ph.D.*	5.00
____ MODERN HYPNOSIS *Lesley Kuhn & Salvatore Russo, Ph.D.*	5.00
____ NEW CONCEPTS OF HYPNOSIS *Bernard C. Gindes, M.D.*	7.00
____ NEW SELF-HYPNOSIS *Paul Adams*	5.00
____ POST-HYPNOTIC INSTRUCTIONS—Suggestions for Therapy *Arnold Furst*	5.00
____ PRACTICAL GUIDE TO SELF-HYPNOSIS *Melvin Powers*	3.00
____ PRACTICAL HYPNOTISM *Philip Magonet, M.D.*	3.00
____ SECRETS OF HYPNOTISM *S. J. Van Pelt, M.D.*	5.00
____ SELF-HYPNOSIS A Conditioned-Response Technique *Laurence Sparks*	7.00
____ SELF-HYPNOSIS Its Theory, Technique & Application *Melvin Powers*	3.00
____ THERAPY THROUGH HYPNOSIS *edited by Raphael H. Rhodes*	5.00

JUDAICA

____ MODERN ISRAEL *Lily Edelman*	2.00
____ SERVICE OF THE HEART *Evelyn Garfiel, Ph.D.*	7.00
____ STORY OF ISRAEL IN COINS *Jean & Maurice Gould*	2.00
____ STORY OF ISRAEL IN STAMPS *Maxim & Gabriel Shamir*	1.00
____ TONGUE OF THE PROPHETS *Robert St. John*	7.00

JUST FOR WOMEN

____ COSMOPOLITAN'S GUIDE TO MARVELOUS MEN Fwd. by *Helen Gurley Brown*	3.00
____ COSMOPOLITAN'S HANG-UP HANDBOOK Foreword by *Helen Gurley Brown*	4.00
____ COSMOPOLITAN'S LOVE BOOK—A Guide to Ecstasy in Bed	5.00
____ COSMOPOLITAN'S NEW ETIQUETTE GUIDE Fwd. by *Helen Gurley Brown*	4.00
____ I AM A COMPLEAT WOMAN *Doris Hagopian & Karen O'Connor Sweeney*	3.00
____ JUST FOR WOMEN—A Guide to the Female Body *Richard E. Sand, M.D.*	5.00
____ NEW APPROACHES TO SEX IN MARRIAGE *John E. Eichenlaub, M.D.*	3.00
____ SEXUALLY ADEQUATE FEMALE *Frank S. Caprio, M.D.*	3.00
____ SEXUALLY FULFILLED WOMAN *Dr. Rachel Copelan*	5.00
____ YOUR FIRST YEAR OF MARRIAGE *Dr. Tom McGinnis*	3.00

MARRIAGE, SEX & PARENTHOOD

____ ABILITY TO LOVE *Dr. Allan Fromme*	6.00
____ GUIDE TO SUCCESSFUL MARRIAGE *Drs. Albert Ellis & Robert Harper*	5.00
____ HOW TO RAISE AN EMOTIONALLY HEALTHY, HAPPY CHILD *A. Ellis*	5.00
____ SEX WITHOUT GUILT *Albert Ellis, Ph.D.*	5.00

____ SEXUALLY ADEQUATE MALE *Frank S. Caprio, M.D.*		3.00
____ SEXUALLY FULFILLED MAN *Dr. Rachel Copelan*		5.00
____ STAYING IN LOVE *Dr. Norton F. Kristy*		7.00

MELVIN POWERS' MAIL ORDER LIBRARY

____ HOW TO GET RICH IN MAIL ORDER *Melvin Powers*		20.00
____ HOW TO WRITE A GOOD ADVERTISEMENT *Victor O. Schwab*		20.00
____ MAIL ORDER MADE EASY *J. Frank Brumbaugh*		10.00
____ U.S. MAIL ORDER SHOPPER'S GUIDE *Susan Spitzer*		10.00

METAPHYSICS & OCCULT

____ BOOK OF TALISMANS, AMULETS & ZODIACAL GEMS *William Pavitt*		7.00
____ CONCENTRATION—A Guide to Mental Mastery *Mouni Sadhu*		5.00
____ CRITIQUES OF GOD *Edited by Peter Angeles*		7.00
____ EXTRA-TERRESTRIAL INTELLIGENCE—The First Encounter		6.00
____ FORTUNE TELLING WITH CARDS *P. Foli*		5.00
____ HANDWRITING ANALYSIS MADE EASY *John Marley*		5.00
____ HANDWRITING TELLS *Nadya Olyanova*		7.00
____ HOW TO INTERPRET DREAMS, OMENS & FORTUNE TELLING SIGNS *Gettings*		5.00
____ HOW TO UNDERSTAND YOUR DREAMS *Geoffrey A. Dudley*		3.00
____ ILLUSTRATED YOGA *William Zorn*		3.00
____ IN DAYS OF GREAT PEACE *Mouni Sadhu*		3.00
____ LSD—THE AGE OF MIND *Bernard Roseman*		2.00
____ MAGICIAN—His Training and Work *W. E. Butler*		3.00
____ MEDITATION *Mouni Sadhu*		7.00
____ MODERN NUMEROLOGY *Morris C. Goodman*		5.00
____ NUMEROLOGY—ITS FACTS AND SECRETS *Ariel Yvon Taylor*		3.00
____ NUMEROLOGY MADE EASY *W. Mykian*		5.00
____ PALMISTRY MADE EASY *Fred Gettings*		5.00
____ PALMISTRY MADE PRACTICAL *Elizabeth Daniels Squire*		5.00
____ PALMISTRY SECRETS REVEALED *Henry Frith*		4.00
____ PROPHECY IN OUR TIME *Martin Ebon*		2.50
____ PSYCHOLOGY OF HANDWRITING *Nadya Olyanova*		7.00
____ SUPERSTITION—Are You Superstitious? *Eric Maple*		2.00
____ TAROT *Mouni Sadhu*		8.00
____ TAROT OF THE BOHEMIANS *Papus*		7.00
____ WAYS TO SELF-REALIZATION *Mouni Sadhu*		3.00
____ WHAT YOUR HANDWRITING REVEALS *Albert E. Hughes*		3.00
____ WITCHCRAFT, MAGIC & OCCULTISM—A Fascinating History *W. B. Crow*		5.00
____ WITCHCRAFT—THE SIXTH SENSE *Justine Glass*		7.00
____ WORLD OF PSYCHIC RESEARCH *Hereward Carrington*		2.00

SELF-HELP & INSPIRATIONAL

____ DAILY POWER FOR JOYFUL LIVING *Dr. Donald Curtis*		5.00
____ DYNAMIC THINKING *Melvin Powers*		5.00
____ GREATEST POWER IN THE UNIVERSE *U. S. Andersen*		5.00
____ GROW RICH WHILE YOU SLEEP *Ben Sweetland*		3.00
____ GROWTH THROUGH REASON *Albert Ellis, Ph.D.*		7.00
____ GUIDE TO PERSONAL HAPPINESS *Albert Ellis, Ph.D. & Irving Becker, Ed. D.*		5.00
____ HELPING YOURSELF WITH APPLIED PSYCHOLOGY *R. Henderson*		2.00
____ HOW TO ATTRACT GOOD LUCK *A. H. Z. Carr*		5.00
____ HOW TO BE GREAT *Dr. Donald Curtis*		5.00
____ HOW TO DEVELOP A WINNING PERSONALITY *Martin Panzer*		5.00
____ HOW TO DEVELOP AN EXCEPTIONAL MEMORY *Young & Gibson*		5.00
____ HOW TO LIVE WITH A NEUROTIC *Albert Ellis, Ph. D.*		5.00
____ HOW TO OVERCOME YOUR FEARS *M. P. Leahy, M.D.*		3.00
____ HOW TO SUCCEED *Brian Adams*		7.00
____ HUMAN PROBLEMS & HOW TO SOLVE THEM *Dr. Donald Curtis*		5.00
____ I CAN *Ben Sweetland*		7.00
____ I WILL *Ben Sweetland*		3.00
____ LEFT-HANDED PEOPLE *Michael Barsley*		5.00
____ MAGIC IN YOUR MIND *U. S. Andersen*		7.00
____ MAGIC OF THINKING BIG *Dr. David J. Schwartz*		3.00

____ MAGIC POWER OF YOUR MIND *Walter M. Germain*		7.00
____ MENTAL POWER THROUGH SLEEP SUGGESTION *Melvin Powers*		3.00
____ NEVER UNDERESTIMATE THE SELLING POWER OF A WOMAN *Dottie Walters*		7.00
____ NEW GUIDE TO RATIONAL LIVING *Albert Ellis, Ph.D. & R. Harper, Ph.D.*		3.00
____ PROJECT YOU *A Manual of Rational Assertiveness Training Paris & Casey*		6.00
____ PSYCHO-CYBERNETICS *Maxwell Maltz, M.D.*		5.00
____ SALES CYBERNETICS *Brian Adams*		7.00
____ SCIENCE OF MIND IN DAILY LIVING *Dr. Donald Curtis*		5.00
____ SECRET OF SECRETS *U. S. Andersen*		7.00
____ SECRET POWER OF THE PYRAMIDS *U. S. Andersen*		7.00
____ SELF-THERAPY FOR THE STUTTERER *Malcolm Fraser*		3.00
____ STUTTERING AND WHAT YOU CAN DO ABOUT IT *W. Johnson, Ph.D.*		2.50
____ SUCCESS-CYBERNETICS *U. S. Andersen*		6.00
____ 10 DAYS TO A GREAT NEW LIFE *William E. Edwards*		3.00
____ THINK AND GROW RICH *Napoleon Hill*		5.00
____ THINK YOUR WAY TO SUCCESS *Dr. Lew Losoncy*		5.00
____ THREE MAGIC WORDS *U. S. Andersen*		7.00
____ TREASURY OF COMFORT *edited by Rabbi Sidney Greenberg*		5.00
____ TREASURY OF THE ART OF LIVING *Sidney S. Greenberg*		5.00
____ YOU ARE NOT THE TARGET *Laura Huxley*		5.00
____ YOUR SUBCONSCIOUS POWER *Charles M. Simmons*		5.00
____ YOUR THOUGHTS CAN CHANGE YOUR LIFE *Dr. Donald Curtis*		5.00

SPORTS

____ BICYCLING FOR FUN AND GOOD HEALTH *Kenneth E. Luther*		2.00
____ BILLIARDS—Pocket • Carom • Three Cushion *Clive Cottingham, Jr.*		5.00
____ CAMPING-OUT 101 Ideas & Activities *Bruno Knobel*		2.00
____ COMPLETE GUIDE TO FISHING *Vlad Evanoff*		2.00
____ HOW TO IMPROVE YOUR RACQUETBALL *Lubarsky Kaufman & Scagnetti*		3.00
____ HOW TO WIN AT POCKET BILLIARDS *Edward D. Knuchell*		5.00
____ JOY OF WALKING *Jack Scagnetti*		3.00
____ LEARNING & TEACHING SOCCER SKILLS *Eric Worthington*		3.00
____ MOTORCYCLING FOR BEGINNERS *I. G. Edmonds*		3.00
____ RACQUETBALL FOR WOMEN *Toni Hudson, Jack Scagnetti & Vince Rondone*		3.00
____ RACQUETBALL MADE EASY *Steve Lubarsky, Rod Delson & Jack Scagnetti*		5.00
____ SECRET OF BOWLING STRIKES *Dawson Taylor*		5.00
____ SECRET OF PERFECT PUTTING *Horton Smith & Dawson Taylor*		5.00
____ SOCCER—The Game & How to Play It *Gary Rosenthal*		5.00
____ STARTING SOCCER *Edward F. Dolan, Jr.*		3.00

TENNIS LOVERS' LIBRARY

____ BEGINNER'S GUIDE TO WINNING TENNIS *Helen Hull Jacobs*		2.00
____ HOW TO BEAT BETTER TENNIS PLAYERS *Loring Fiske*		4.00
____ HOW TO IMPROVE YOUR TENNIS—Style, Strategy & Analysis *C. Wilson*		2.00
____ PLAY TENNIS WITH ROSEWALL *Ken Rosewall*		2.00
____ PSYCH YOURSELF TO BETTER TENNIS *Dr. Walter A. Luszki*		2.00
____ TENNIS FOR BEGINNERS, *Dr. H. A. Murray*		2.00
____ TENNIS MADE EASY *Joel Brecheen*		4.00
____ WEEKEND TENNIS—How to Have Fun & Win at the Same Time *Bill Talbert*		3.00
____ WINNING WITH PERCENTAGE TENNIS—Smart Strategy *Jack Lowe*		2.00

WILSHIRE PET LIBRARY

____ DOG OBEDIENCE TRAINING *Gust Kessopulos*		5.00
____ DOG TRAINING MADE EASY & FUN *John W. Kellogg*		4.00
____ HOW TO BRING UP YOUR PET DOG *Kurt Unkelbach*		2.00
____ HOW TO RAISE & TRAIN YOUR PUPPY *Jeff Griffen*		5.00
____ PIGEONS: HOW TO RAISE & TRAIN THEM *William H. Allen, Jr.*		2.00

*The books listed above can be obtained from your book dealer or directly from
Melvin Powers. When ordering, please remit $1.00 postage for the first book
and 50¢ for each additional book.*

Melvin Powers

12015 Sherman Road, No. Hollywood, California 91605